HTML
FOR
DUMMIES®

Quick Reference

2nd Edition

by Deborah S. Ray and
Eric J. Ray

D0003226

IDG
BOOKS
WORLDWIDE

IDG Books Worldwide, Inc.
An International Data Group Company

Foster City, CA ✦ Chicago, IL ✦ Indianapolis, IN ✦ Southlake, TX

HTML For Dummies® Quick Reference, 2nd Edition

Published by
IDG Books Worldwide, Inc.
An International Data Group Company
919 E. Hillsdale Blvd.
Suite 400
Foster City, CA 94404
www.idgbooks.com (IDG Books Worldwide Web site)
www.dummies.com (Dummies Press Web site)

Library of Congress Catalog Card No.: 97-72401

ISBN: 0-7645-0248-4

Printed in the United States of America

10 9 8 7 6 5 4 3

2P/SU/RR/ZX/IN

Distributed in the United States by IDG Books Worldwide, Inc.

Distributed by Macmillan Canada for Canada; by Transworld Publishers Limited in the United Kingdom; by IDG Norge Books for Norway; by IDG Sweden Books for Sweden; by Woodslane Pty. Ltd. for Australia; by Woodslane Enterprises Ltd. for New Zealand; by Longman Singapore Publishers Ltd. for Singapore, Malaysia, Thailand, and Indonesia; by Simron Pty. Ltd. for South Africa; by Toppan Company Ltd. for Japan; by Distribuidora Cuspide for Argentina; by Livraria Cultura for Brazil; by Ediciencia S.A. for Ecuador; by Addison-Wesley Publishing Company for Korea; by Ediciones ZETA S.C.R. Ltda. for Peru; by WS Computer Publishing Corporation, Inc., for the Philippines; by Unalis Corporation for Taiwan; by Contemporanea de Ediciones for Venezuela; by Computer Book & Magazine Store for Puerto Rico; by Express Computer Distributors for the Caribbean and West Indies. Authorized Sales Agent: Anthony Rudkin Associates for the Middle East and North Africa.

For general information on IDG Books Worldwide's books in the U.S., please call our Consumer Customer Service department at 800-762-2974. For reseller information, including discounts and premium sales, please call our Reseller Customer Service department at 800-434-3422.

For information on where to purchase IDG Books Worldwide's books outside the U.S., please contact our International Sales department at 415-655-3200 or fax 415-655-3295.

For information on foreign language translations, please contact our Foreign & Subsidiary Rights department at 415-655-3021 or fax 415-655-3281.

For sales inquiries and special prices for bulk quantities, please contact our Sales department at 415-655-3200 or write to the address above.

For information on using IDG Books Worldwide's books in the classroom or for ordering examination copies, please contact our Educational Sales department at 800-434-2086 or fax 817-251-8174.

For press review copies, author interviews, or other publicity information, please contact our Public Relations department at 415-655-3000 or fax 415-655-3299.

For authorization to photocopy items for corporate, personal, or educational use, please contact Copyright Clearance Center, 222 Rosewood Drive, Danvers, MA 01923, or fax 508-750-4470.

is a trademark under exclusive license to IDG Books Worldwide, Inc., from International Data Group, Inc.

About the Authors

Just a word about us — so that you know who the "we" is that we refer to throughout this book.

We are Deborah and Eric Ray, owners of RayComm, Inc., a technical communication consulting company. For the most part, we write computer books, including *Dummies 101: HTML* and *Approach 97 For Windows For Dummies,* to name a couple. In fact, (if you can pardon a little bragging) *HTML For Dummies Quick Reference* (this book's 1st edition) and *Dummies 101: HTML* won international awards at the 1996 Society for Technical Communication Technical Publications Competition. And, when we're not trapped under mounds of book drafts, we also give occasional seminars on HTML and Internet-related topics.

I, **Deborah Ray** (my friends call me Deb), have been a technical communicator for the past four years and have been involved with the Internet for the past three years. I teach technical writing to students at Utah State University and have taught the same at Oklahoma State University. I also have a variety of technical experience, including creating various computer and engineering documents for a variety of audiences. My areas of emphasis include writing, designing, and illustrating documents to meet various audiences' information needs.

I, **Eric Ray** (my friends call me, well, Eric), have been involved with the Internet for five years and have made numerous presentations and written several papers about HTML and online information. (I like to hear myself write.) My technical experience includes creating and maintaining the TECHWR-L listserv list (a discussion forum for technical communications) as well as implementing and running Web servers. I guess you'd say that I'm a Webmaster. As a technical communicator, I focus on making "techie" information easy for normal people to understand.

Thanks to our combined skills, we've reached stereotypical *geek* status, having side-by-side home computer workstations at which we work hours and hours every day. Our cats perch on the monitors, stare at us, and attempt to supervise our work. (Actually, we think they're just keeping their tummies warm.)

ABOUT IDG BOOKS WORLDWIDE

Welcome to the world of IDG Books Worldwide.

IDG Books Worldwide, Inc., is a subsidiary of International Data Group, the world's largest publisher of computer-related information and the leading global provider of information services on information technology. IDG was founded more than 25 years ago and now employs more than 8,500 people worldwide. IDG publishes more than 275 computer publications in over 75 countries (see listing below). More than 60 million people read one or more IDG publications each month.

Launched in 1990, IDG Books Worldwide is today the #1 publisher of best-selling computer books in the United States. We are proud to have received eight awards from the Computer Press Association in recognition of editorial excellence and three from *Computer Currents'* First Annual Readers' Choice Awards. Our best-selling *...For Dummies*® series has more than 30 million copies in print with translations in 30 languages. IDG Books Worldwide, through a joint venture with IDG's Hi-Tech Beijing, became the first U.S. publisher to publish a computer book in the People's Republic of China. In record time, IDG Books Worldwide has become the first choice for millions of readers around the world who want to learn how to better manage their businesses.

Our mission is simple: Every one of our books is designed to bring extra value and skill-building instructions to the reader. Our books are written by experts who understand and care about our readers. The knowledge base of our editorial staff comes from years of experience in publishing, education, and journalism — experience we use to produce books for the '90s. In short, we care about books, so we attract the best people. We devote special attention to details such as audience, interior design, use of icons, and illustrations. And because we use an efficient process of authoring, editing, and desktop publishing our books electronically, we can spend more time ensuring superior content and spend less time on the technicalities of making books.

You can count on our commitment to deliver high-quality books at competitive prices on topics you want to read about. At IDG Books Worldwide, we continue in the IDG tradition of delivering quality for more than 25 years. You'll find no better book on a subject than one from IDG Books Worldwide.

IDG BOOKS
WORLDWIDE

John Kilcullen
John Kilcullen
CEO
IDG Books Worldwide, Inc.

Steven Berkowitz
Steven Berkowitz
President and Publisher
IDG Books Worldwide, Inc.

IDG Books Worldwide, Inc., is a subsidiary of International Data Group, the world's largest publisher of computer-related information and the leading global provider of information services on information technology. International Data Group publishes over 275 computer publications in over 75 countries. Sixty million people read one or more International Data Group publications each month. International Data Group's publications include: ARGENTINA: Buyer's Guide, Computerworld Argentina, PC World Argentina; AUSTRALIA: Australian Macworld, Australian PC World, Australian Reseller News, Computerworld, IT Casebook, Network World, Publish, Webmaster; AUSTRIA: Computerwelt Osterreich, Networks Austria, PC Tip Austria; BANGLADESH: PC World Bangladesh; BELARUS: PC World Belarus; BELGIUM: Data News; BRAZIL: Annuario de Informatica, Computerworld, Connections, Macworld, PC Player, PC World, Publish, Reseller News, Supergamepower; BULGARIA: Computerworld Bulgaria, Network World Bulgaria, PC & MacWorld Bulgaria; CANADA: CIO Canada, Client/Server World, ComputerWorld Canada, InfoWorld Canada, NetworkWorld Canada, WebWorld; CHILE: Computerworld Chile, PC World Chile; COLOMBIA: Computerworld Colombia, PC World Colombia; COSTA RICA: PC World Centro America; THE CZECH AND SLOVAK REPUBLICS: Computerworld Czechoslovakia, Macworld Czech Republic, PC World Czechoslovakia; DENMARK: Communications World Danmark, Computerworld Danmark, Macworld Danmark, PC World Danmark, Techworld Denmark; DOMINICAN REPUBLIC: PC World Republica Dominicana; ECUADOR: PC World Ecuador; EGYPT: Computerworld Middle East, PC World Middle East; EL SALVADOR: PC World Centro America; FINLAND: MikroPC, Tietoverkko, Tietoviikko; FRANCE: Distributique, Hebdo, Info PC, Le Monde Informatique, Macworld, Reseaux & Telecoms, WebMaster France; GERMANY: Computer Partner, Computerwoche, Computerwoche Extra, Computerwoche FOCUS, Global Online, Macwelt, PC Welt; GREECE: Amiga Computing, GamePro Greece, Multimedia World; GUATEMALA: PC World Centro America; HONDURAS: PC World Centro America; HONG KONG: Computerworld Hong Kong, PC World Hong Kong, Publish in Asia; HUNGARY: ABCD CD-ROM, Computerworld Szamitastechnika, Internetto online Magazine, PC World Hungary, PC-X Magazin Hungary; ICELAND: Tolvuheimur PC World Island; INDIA: Information Communications World, Information Systems Computerworld, PC World India, Publish in Asia; INDONESIA: InfoKomputer PC World, Komputek Computerworld, Publish in Asia; IRELAND: ComputerScope, PC Live!; ISRAEL: Macworld Israel, People & Computers/Computerworld; ITALY: Computerworld Italia, Macworld Italia, Networking Italia, PC World Italia; JAPAN: DTP World, Macworld Japan, Nikkei Personal Computing, OS/2 Japan, SunWorld Japan, Windows NT World, Windows World Japan; KENYA: PC World East African; KOREA: Hi-Tech Information, Macworld Korea, PC World Korea; MACEDONIA: PC World Macedonia; MALAYSIA: Computerworld Malaysia, PC World Malaysia, Publish in Asia; MALTA: PC World Malta; MEXICO: Computerworld Mexico, PC World Mexico; MYANMAR: PC World Myanmar; NETHERLANDS: Computer! Totaal, LAN Internetworking Magazine, LAN World Buyers Guide, Macworld Netherlands, Net, WebWereld; NEW ZEALAND: Absolute Beginners Guide and Plain & Simple Series, Computer Buyer, Computer Industry Directory, Computerworld New Zealand, MTB, Network World, PC World New Zealand; NICARAGUA: PC World Centro America; NORWAY: Computerworld Norge, CW Rapport, Datamagasinet, Financial Rapport, Kursguide Norge, Macworld Norge, Multimediaworld Norge, PC World Ekspress Norge, PC World Nettverk, PC World Norge, PC World ProduktGuide Norge; PAKISTAN: Computerworld Pakistan; PANAMA: PC World Panama; PEOPLE'S REPUBLIC OF CHINA: China Computer Users, China Computerworld, China InfoWorld, China Telecom World Weekly, Computer & Communication, Electronic Design China, Electronics Today, Electronics Weekly, Game Software, PC World China, Popular Computer Week, Software Weekly, Software World, Telecom World; PERU: Computerworld Peru, PC World Profesional Peru, PC World SoHo Peru; PHILIPPINES: Click!, Computerworld Philippines, PC World Philippines, Publish in Asia; POLAND: Computerworld Poland, Computerworld Special Report Poland, Cyber, Macworld Poland, Networld Poland, PC World Komputer; PORTUGAL: Cerebro/PC World, Computerworld/Correio Informático, Dealer World Portugal, Mac*In/PC*In Portugal, Multimedia World; PUERTO RICO: PC World Puerto Rico; ROMANIA: Computerworld Romania, PC World Romania, Telecom Romania; RUSSIA: Computerworld Russia, Mir PK, Publish, Seti; SINGAPORE: Computerworld Singapore, PC World Singapore, Publish in Asia; SLOVENIA: Monitor; SOUTH AFRICA: Computing SA, Network World SA, Software World SA; SPAIN: Communicaciones World España, Computerworld España, Dealer World España, Macworld España, PC World España; SRI LANKA: Infolink PC World; SWEDEN: CAP&Design, Computer Sweden, Corporate Computing Sweden, Internetworld Sweden, it branschen, Macworld Sweden, MaxiData Sweden, MikroDatorn, Natverk & Kommunikation, PC World Sweden, PCaktiv, Windows World Sweden; SWITZERLAND: Computerworld Schweiz, Macworld Schweiz, PCtip; TAIWAN: Computerworld Taiwan, Macworld Taiwan, NEW ViSiON/Publish, PC World Taiwan, Windows World Taiwan; THAILAND: Publish in Asia, Thai Computerworld; TURKEY: Computerworld Turkiye, Macworld Turkiye, Network World Turkiye, PC World Turkiye; UKRAINE: Computerworld Kiev, Multimedia World Ukraine, PC World Ukraine; UNITED KINGDOM: Acorn User UK, Amiga Action UK, Amiga Computing UK, Apple Talk UK, Computing, Macworld, Parents and Computers UK, PC Advisor, PC Home, PSX Pro, The WEB; UNITED STATES: Cable in the Classroom, CIO Magazine, Computerworld, DOS World, Federal Computer Week, GamePro Magazine, InfoWorld, I-Way, Macworld, Network World, PC Games, PC World, Publish, Video Event, THE WEB Magazine, and WebMaster; online webzines: JavaWorld, NetscapeWorld, and SunWorld Online; URUGUAY: InfoWorld Uruguay; VENEZUELA: Computerworld Venezuela, PC World Venezuela; and VIETNAM: PC World Vietnam.   3/24/97

Dedication

To each other . . . and Ashleigh.

Acknowledgments

We owe many people a big round of thanks for helping us complete this book. We are most grateful to Gareth Hancock, acquisitions editor at IDG Books Worldwide, Inc., for his continued confidence in us. A special thanks to Rev Mengle, project editor, for his guidance and contributions to our work, as well as to Melba Hopper, who helped us develop this book in the first place.

We also want to thank the whole crew of people at IDG Books who helped produce this book. A big thank you goes to our copy editor, William A. Barton, and to our technical editor, James Michael Stewart. We also send our appreciation to the book's indexer and to the entire production team. Each of these highly competent people contributed a great deal to this book — and to our sanity.

We'd like to extend our special appreciation to some folks at two universities. First, thanks to the faculty of the Utah State University (USU) Technical Writing Program for welcoming us to the neighborhood and for providing us with exciting new opportunities. Second, thanks to the faculty of the Oklahoma State University (OSU) Technical Writing Program for their support and encouragement over the years. And thanks to OSU's Computing and Information Services for supporting Eric's insatiable appetite for technology, which helped provide a foundation for pursuing this book.

Finally, a great big ol' thanks to Megg Bonar, former acquisitions editor at IDG Books, for the "foot-in-the-door" and the kind notes left in her desk.

Publisher's Acknowledgments

We're proud of this book; please register your comments through our IDG Books Worldwide Online Registration Form located at: http://my2cents.dummies.com.

Some of the people who helped bring this book to market include the following:

Acquisitions, Development, and Editorial

Project Editors: Rev Mengle, Melba Hopper

Acquisitions Editor: Michael Kelly

Media Development Manager: Joyce Pepple

Copy Editors: William A. Barton, John C. Edwards, Suzanne Thomas, Joe Jansen

Technical Reviewer: James Michael Stewart

Editorial Managers: Mary C. Corder, Seta Frantz

Editorial Assistant: Darren Meiss

Production

Project Coordinator: Debbie Stailey

Layout and Graphics: Cameron Booker, Elizabeth Cárdenas-Nelson, Todd Klemme, Brent Savage, M. Anne Sipahimalani, Kate Snell

Proofreaders: Sharon Duffy, Kelli Botta, Joel K. Draper, Robert Springer

Indexer: Lori Lathrop

Special Help

Colleen Rainsberger, Senior Project Editor; Chris H. Collins, Editorial Assistant; Jerelind Charles, Editorial Assistant; Tamara S. Castleman, Senior Copy Editor; Stephanie Koutek, Proof Editor

---

General and Administrative

IDG Books Worldwide, Inc.: John Kilcullen, CEO; Steven Berkowitz, President and Publisher

IDG Books Technology Publishing: Brenda McLaughlin, Senior Vice President and Group Publisher

Dummies Technology Press and Dummies Editorial: Diane Graves Steele, Vice President and Associate Publisher; Mary Bednarek, Acquisitions and Product Development Director; Kristin A. Cocks, Editorial Director

Dummies Trade Press: Kathleen A. Welton, Vice President and Publisher; Kevin Thornton, Acquisitions Manager

IDG Books Production for Dummies Press: Beth Jenkins, Production Director; Cindy L. Phipps, Manager of Project Coordination, Production Proofreading, and Indexing; Kathie S. Schutte, Supervisor of Page Layout; Shelley Lea, Supervisor of Graphics and Design; Debbie J. Gates, Production Systems Specialist; Robert Springer, Supervisor of Proofreading; Debbie Stailey, Special Projects Coordinator; Tony Augsburger, Supervisor of Reprints and Bluelines; Leslie Popplewell, Media Archive Coordinator

Dummies Packaging and Book Design: Patti Crane, Packaging Specialist; Lance Kayser, Packaging Assistant; Kavish + Kavish, Cover Design

♦

The publisher would like to give special thanks to Patrick J. McGovern, without whom this book would not have been possible.

♦

Table of Contents

How to Use This Book

We want you to do something very important with this book — keep it off the shelf, on your desk, and on top of your piles of papers. If you follow the guidelines presented in this book, you're going to be well on your way to producing those nifty HTML documents that everyone is talking about.

This little book doesn't contain everything you can possibly know about HTML, but it does provide the information that you need to produce quality, usable HTML documents. Our goal is to provide you with information that enables you to create HTML documents correctly and quickly — without pulling your hair out.

We take a very practical approach to using HTML. You don't find a lot of unnecessary theory. Instead, you find how-to information, examples, and tips that help you create a variety of HTML documents and applications.

The information in this book applies to Windows (3.x, 95, and NT), Macintosh, and UNIX users, as well as almost every other computer demographic. Because HTML isn't platform-specific, we aren't either. In some places, we assume that you know what software you're using. Don't worry, however — just substitute the actual name of your software for the phrase "your software."

Happy HTML authoring and good luck!

How This Book Is Organized

This book is organized so that you can find information by browsing through the sections or by looking in the Table of Contents and the Index. If you're looking for specific information, notice that, within each part, the major headings in each section are alphabetically arranged. If you're looking for a general introduction to HTML, you can start at the beginning of this book and work your way through. By browsing through the various sections, you get an idea of the types of things you can do by using HTML. In the Table of Contents and the Index, you can look up specific information.

Please pay particular attention to the introductory pages for the parts in this book. Those pages tell you what you need to know before you can successfully complete the tasks in the parts.

What You Need to Know

Creating HTML documents isn't at all difficult after you get the hang of it, but you do need to pay special attention to a few points of interest.

Creating HTML documents

To create an HTML document, you must use a text editor in which to enter the HTML and a browser with which to view your success. You can use Notepad (for Windows 3.x, Windows 95, or Windows NT), SimpleText or TeachText (for Macintosh), pico or vi (for UNIX), or whatever plain-text editor you're most comfortable with.

After you begin doing HTML documents — or if you want to make your life as easy as possible — check out some of the specialized HTML editing programs available in software stores and on the Internet. These programs range from the relatively simple (Netscape Composer, WebEdit) to the high-end and complex (Microsoft Front Page, Adobe PageMill, NetObjects Fusion). The more specialized programs can automate a lot of the typing and tagging you must otherwise do yourself.

Saving your documents

After you create an HTML document, save it somewhere on your computer. Where you put the document really doesn't matter, but you usually find that putting all these files in the same folder (or directory) is the easiest approach.

If you use a word processor such as Word or WordPerfect, you must save all your documents as plain-text or as ASCII files (they're the same thing). Remember, too, that the last part of the document name must be .htm or .html. (Older DOS/Windows 3.x computers can't handle more than three characters in the extension, so for these computers, use .htm.)

Viewing your documents

Whenever you're ready to take a peek at your HTML documents, just use the following procedure.

Note: For those who prefer using keyboard shortcuts to mousing around, we indicate the shortcuts by underlining the keys to press.

Follow these steps:

1. Open your browser (Netscape Navigator, Internet Explorer, or whatever).

2. Choose File⇨Open File (or File⇨Open or something similar, depending on the version of the program that you have) and open somefile.htm or whatever file you're working on.

3. Check to see whether your document looks as you think it should.

4. Make changes to the document in your text editor and save the document.

5. Return to the browser and click your Reload or Refresh button.

   This step reloads the file. You're ready to perform Step 3 again.

What's in This Book?

This book contains eight parts, two appendixes, and a glossary.

The **Introduction** (which, of course, you're now reading) contains information about what this book does and doesn't include and information about the icons and conventions used in this book, as well as a call for your feedback.

Part I, "Answering the Basic Questions about HTML," does exactly what it says by focusing on how HTML applies to you. This material isn't as theoretical as it may sound — a better understanding of a few of the basics before you dive in may make the whole process flow more easily.

Part II, "Creating an HTML Page," gets you started developing basic HTML documents. You find many examples, pictures, and step-by-step instructions to help you. A tip for the eager: The fun stuff starts here.

Part III, "Spinning Your HTML Web," discusses the ins and outs of URLs, which are the addresses that describe locations of documents and other files on the Internet (or more specifically, the World Wide Web). We give the steps you need to link your HTML document to other files on the Web.

Part IV, "Using Images in Your Web Pages," shows you how to include graphics in your HTML document. This part tells you what kinds of graphics you can use and how to put them in your page. You also find examples, pictures, and step-by-step instructions in this part.

Part V, "Making Effective Web Pages," shows you how to make eye-catching, usable HTML documents. This part helps you create HTML documents that everyone wants to read and prevents you from creating examples for the "Ten Things Not to Do with a Web Page" list.

Part VI, "Serving HTML to the World," tells you how to make your HTML documents available to the world. You're not going to keep your documents to yourself, are you? This part focuses on the pros, cons, and how-tos of putting your stuff out on the Web.

Part VII, "Framing Your Site," gives you all the information you need to use frames in your Web site, including the tags and attributes, as well as a number of tips to make the process easier.

Part VIII, "Developing Your Web Site — Putting It All Together," focuses on the do's and don'ts of writing and designing Web Pages and provides information about the process you can follow to create effective Web sites.

Appendix A, "HTML Tags," provides a list of HTML commands. In addition to the commands introduced throughout this book, you find scads more to add to your repertoire as you advance your skills.

Appendix B, "Special Symbols," provides you with a list of symbols that you can include in an HTML document. Browse through this section to see all the neat symbols you can include.

The **Glossary,** "Techie Talk," contains an alphabetical listing of peculiar terms used throughout this book. If you can never remember what FTP, HTML, and URL stand for, the Glossary is an easy place to find out.

What's Not in This Book?

This book focuses on showing you how to use HTML; it doesn't, however, cover a few relevant topics in depth — for example, using text editors, using a browser, using FTP, and using graphics programs. "Creating HTML Documents," in Part I, touches on these subjects, but it doesn't provide the how-to information that you may need.

If you need help using text editors, browsers, FTP, or graphics software, you have a few choices. First, you may want to get *The Internet For Dummies*, 4th Edition, by John R. Levine, Carol Baroudi, and Margaret Levine Young (published by IDG Books Worldwide, Inc.). Second, consider getting the relevant *...For Dummies* book for your platform — choose from *Windows 95 For Dummies,* 2nd Edition, or *Windows 3.11 For Dummies,* 3rd Edition, by Andy Rathbone; *UNIX For Dummies,* 3rd Edition, by John Levine; or *Macs For Dummies,* 5th Edition, by David Pogue. Or you can try asking your local computer geek (who, of course, already has the complete *...For Dummies* series).

Second, you can get all the information you want on the Internet by searching in your current favorite index or directory (we like Yahoo! at http://www.yahoo.com and AltaVista at http://www.altavista.digital.com/) for terms such as HTML, graphics, or browser. From these terms, you can find your way to loads of additional information about HTML and related topics.

Third, co-workers (with the propeller beanies) or the children of co-workers are also good bets. Don't ask your own kids — they're likely to laugh at you, and you can never get any respect from them afterward.

In any case, if you're a beginner, don't be afraid to ask questions such as the following:

✦ Would you help me find my Web browser and tell me what it's called?

✦ What kinds of text editors do I have on my computer?

✦ Do I have any graphics programs that I can use to create a GIF (pronounced like *jif* in jiffy or *gif* in gift — take your pick) or a JPG *(jay-peg)* file? Don't worry; if you check out Part IV before you ask, you're even going to know what you're talking about.

Meet the Icon Crew

Throughout this book, we include a variety of icons that help point out important information, provide helpful hints, or show an easier way of doing things.

This icon indicates that you need to ask for assistance from your server administrator (aka Web administrator or Webmaster) to complete the task. This icon is used where the required information varies according to how the administrator set up the Web server that you use.

This icon marks places where we provide references to other sources that may help you — although this book is packed full of useful information, we can't possibly include everything you want to know.

This icon points to examples throughout this book. By trying them out on your own computer, you can become proficient with using HTML.

This icon provides little reminders that help you avoid common mistakes — particularly ones that we make. So if that darned thing just doesn't work, check your document for information noted by this icon.

This icon shows where we provide information that can help you become better users of HTML.

Conventions Used in This Book

To help keep things as consistent as possible, we provide a few stylistic conventions.

Where we want you to try out HTML examples that we provide, we place the commands that you enter on a separate line in a special typeface or in boldface within a step. Those commands on separate lines look similar to the following example:

```
<A>Cats</A> are funny.
```

Or, inside a step, what you enter appears as shown in the following example:

1. Enter **Cats are funny** between the <BODY> tags.

Note: Make sure that you type the commands exactly as they appear.

Sometimes we provide an extended example with just a little new text within it. The extra text helps you get your bearings within the larger context. We put the new stuff in boldface so that you can see what to type or what's been changed, as in this example:

```
<A>Cats</A> are funny, usually.
```

Several times throughout the book, we use "*Note:*", which always appears in boldface and italics. Primarily, we use *Note:* to indicate what software or files you need to have open before starting an example. Additionally, we use *Note:* to emphasize information (as it does for the information that appears after the sample step a few paragraphs ago).

In many places, we include tables with HTML tags. These tables are always formatted in the same way, as follows:

✦ The first column provides the specific HTML tag or attribute — tags are enclosed in pointed brackets (⟨ ⟩); attributes appear in *italics*.

✦ The second column provides a description of each tag and attribute.

✦ The third column provides additional information.

In several places, we provide you with a series of steps to complete in a certain order, as follows:

1. These steps appear in numbered lists.

2. Completing each step in order is important.

3. Please complete these steps in the order specified.

In other places, we provide you with bulleted lists, similar to the following:

✦ Some of these lists provide steps that you can complete in any order.

✦ Others provide descriptive information.

Finally, we provide words in *italics* to indicate the first time that we use a new term or abbreviation. These terms are defined or described where they appear, and we also include them in the Glossary for easy reference.

As you can see after you read a few of the examples in this book, our three cats (Winchester, Lucy, and Booker) figure prominently throughout. They continually offer us inspiration as we figure out lighthearted ways to explain information. As you read the examples, rest assured that we have never and would never consider doing or recommending anything that might harm the cats. Please take these examples as tongue-in-cheek humor, for that's how we intend them.

How Did It Go?

The information in this book can help you develop nifty, eye-catching pages, and we're sure you're going to be a smashing success at creating HTML documents. We'd love to hear your comments and suggestions. Please feel free to contact us by e-mail at debray@raycomm.com or ejray@raycomm.com.

Part 1

Answering the Basic Questions about HTML

Part I covers the *whats, wheres,* and *whys* of HTML —
a great place to get started if you're a complete novice
with this stuff. And even if you already have some clue
as to what HTML is all about, this part can help you
understand how the whole HTML/Intranet/a World
Wide Web/WWW/Web business fits together.

In this part . . .

✔ **Figuring out HTML basics**

✔ **Knowing what you use HTML documents for**

✔ **Creating HTML documents**

✔ **Publishing HTML documents**

✔ **Getting started**

About HTML Basics

HTML is nothing more than the computer language (or gobbledygook, depending on your perspective) that makes World Wide Web pages.

HTML stands for *HyperText Markup Language.* HTML is only text and doesn't actually contain images, video, or sound, although it allows you to include these things in a document. The following list explains exactly what each part of HyperText Markup Language means to you:

✦ *HyperText* allows you to connect to places within a given document, to another page on the same Web site, or to a page located anywhere in the world on another Web site.

HyperText lets you read a document or documents by jumping from one part to another, according to your interests and needs, instead of progressing linearly from the beginning to the end (as when you read a novel).

✦ *Markup Language* is a system of codes (the terms that look like gobbledygook) that identifies logical parts of a document, such as headings, paragraphs, lists, and so on. These codes, referred to as *tags,* name the parts of the document but don't necessarily specify what the parts of the document actually look like. For example, you label the title of your document as follows:

```
<TITLE>Whatever Your Title Is Called</TITLE>
```

By using HTML, you don't need to worry about how to format any part of your document. Just label each document part by applying a tag that indicates what the element is. If you show that an element is a `<TITLE>`, for example, the computer takes care of determining such elements as the font, font size, and emphasis (such as bold or italic). In a sense, using HTML makes creating documents easier because you don't need to choose what you want the parts of the document to look like; you must determine only what the element is.

More recent versions of HTML, however, let you exercise some control over document appearance — almost as much control, in fact, as you could in using a word processing document or a crayon. You can use HTML to specify fonts, font sizes, and color, for example, which come in handy for designing really snazzy Web pages.

HTML was created at the Center for High Energy Physics in Switzerland so that researchers could share their papers *online,* meaning on the computer rather than on paper. Unfortunately, the researchers weren't too interested in fancy formatting or marketing their ideas, so the original version of HTML didn't offer many formatting options. You could create some really neat effects in older versions of HTML, but they took a little extra work and a few odd work-arounds. Now we're benefiting from the marketing savvy of various large corporations that are expanding the standard to include a variety of formatting and display options. If you're using the latest version of the standard, great Web pages literally lie at your fingertips. (Assuming that you're sitting at the computer keyboard, that is.)

Applications for HTML Documents

You use HTML to organize the information in *electronic documents* (as opposed to tree-killing paper ones) so that people can browse through the document by navigating from topic to topic instead of reading from line to line or page to page. Organizing electronic documents is hard to do well, but done well, the process allows users to navigate through information and cross-reference other topics without needing to read through irrelevant, unnecessary, or boring information.

See also Part VIII, Developing Your Web Site — Putting It All Together, which gives you more information about organizing your HTML documents to make them easier for your readers to use.

You use HTML documents for two purposes, the most common of which is developing those nifty pages that you see on the World Wide Web. HTML documents let you easily communicate information you have to anyone in the world who wants or needs it. You may, for example, provide information about your small business to the world or about your hobby to other hobbyists. Either way, by using easy-to-create HTML documents, you can provide an "up-with-technology" look and feel without great expense and years of computer training.

The following screen gives you an example of how Habitat for Humanity uses a Web site to achieve that up-with-technology look and feel.

Another purpose for HTML documents is for developing Web pages that you can publish on a corporate *intranet,* which is a smaller Web that provides information to company employees. By providing information on an intranet, you can give employees schedule updates, publish corporate policies, announce information about groups within MongoCorporation to the other divisions, or give instructions on filling out those dreaded forms. The following screen shows you how ACME Services, Inc., hypothetically publishes information on its intranet, called ACMEnet.

Provide all sorts of information that employees need but that the whole world shouldn't see!

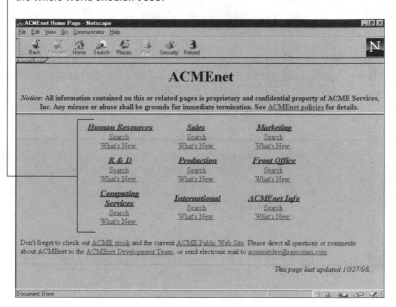

Creating HTML Documents

To create HTML documents, you do need at least two different kinds of software — an editor to create your documents and a browser to view your documents. You're also likely to need some other software — FTP software if you want to put your pages "out there" on the Web and image-editing software if you want to include images in your pages. So if you don't have the software you need, we suggest getting "with the program" by obtaining them from either the Internet or from your favorite computer store.

If you're not quite sure where to start finding and downloading programs from the Internet, check out *The Internet For Dummies,* 4th Edition, by John Levine; *Dummies 101: The Internet For Windows 95,* by Margy Levine Young; *The Internet for Dummies Quick Reference,* 3rd Edition, by John Levine; or *HTML For Dummies,* 3rd Edition, by Ed Tittel and Steve James, all published by IDG Books Worldwide, Inc.

Editors

Editors are programs you use to create HTML documents. To create an HTML document, you can explore (and mix and match) several options, as follows:

✦ You can use a plain old *text editor* that provides you with a place to type your text and tags.

✦ You can use a code-based *HTML editor,* which helps ease the process of creating a document by automating some of the tedious tag-typing. Generally, using an HTML editor is similar to using a plain old text editor, except that the HTML editor has cool buttons that enable you to apply HTML code with a simple click rather than a bunch of typing.

✦ You can use a *WYSIWYG* (What You See Is What You Get) HTML editor, which lets you see the document approximately as it appears in a browser. In most of these editors, you don't see the tags; instead, you just click a formatting button and that action inserts the tags behind the scenes.

✦ You can use a word processing program or any number of programs that offers a *Save As Text* option, just as you would use a text editor.

✦ You can use a word processing program or any number of programs that offer a *Save As HTML* option. The Save As HTML option allows you to convert your documents into HTML so that you can publish them on the Web or on an intranet. Many newer spreadsheet, database, and presentation software packages, for example, enable you to easily save your creation as an HTML document. Additionally, virtually all the newest word processing software packages and desktop publishing packages enable you to save your file in HTML format.

✦ You can use a *converter,* which lets you take an existing document and turn it into an HTML document without much effort.

Each of these choices has certain advantages. The options that enable you to see and manipulate the code, for example, offer you much more control over your final documents. The WYSIWYG options are arguably easier to use, however, and the solutions based on using existing software are certainly the most convenient and quickest for getting a document roughed out.

We've found, particularly given the inherent limitations of HTML, that at some point, you need to work directly with the HTML code to get the results you want. This book focuses on how to understand and work with HTML code to develop Web pages and sites. You don't, however, need to knock yourself out.

If you have a lot of documents to create or to convert to HTML format, do use your word processor or a conversion program to take care of the tedious work for you. We see no point in hand-coding your entire personnel manual into HTML, for example, if you can just choose a Save As HTML command in your word processing program and then use the information in this book to tweak the formatting.

After you gain some experience with HTML, you find that combining several techniques works wonders. We've found, for example, that we're most productive if we use a word processor to get the HTML document to the "close-but-no-cigar" stage and then use a plain text editor or code-based HTML editor to fine-tune it. As they say on the 'Net, however, your mileage may vary. Don't hesitate to try several different systems until you find what works for you.

Here are some good choices for text editors, all of which are available on the specific platforms shown in parentheses:

✦ Notepad (Windows 3.*x*, Windows 95, Windows NT)

✦ TeachText or SimpleText (Macintosh)

✦ vi or pico (UNIX)

Additionally, if you want to seek out programs on the Internet, you may consider code-based HTML editors such as the following:

✦ Hotdog, from Sausage Software at `http://www.sausage.com` (Windows)

✦ WebEdit, from Luckman International at `http://www.sandiego.com/webedit/` (Windows)

✦ BBEdit, from Bare Bones Software at `http://www.barebones.com` (Macintosh)

✦ World Wide Web Weaver at `http://www.miracleinc.com` (Macintosh)

✦ HTML pad, from Intermania Software at `http://www.intermania.com` (Windows)

Browsers

Browsers are the programs that people use to look at HTML documents. Usually, people are referring to their browsers if they talk about their Internet software or their Web client software.

After you create HTML documents with those gobbledygook tags, you want to see what they really look like. You open the documents in your browser, which interprets the HTML tags and displays the documents as they should appear.

Following are a few browsers with which you may be familiar:

✦ Netscape Navigator (Windows, Macintosh, UNIX)

✦ Microsoft Internet Explorer (Windows, Macintosh)

✦ Lynx (text-only interfaces — primarily UNIX)

Keep in mind that different browsers display things differently. If, for example, you create a first-level heading in your HTML document, one browser may display it as 14-point Times New Roman Bold, while another browser may display it as 15-point Arial Bold Italic. Either way, the heading appears as bigger and bolder than normal text, but the specifics of what it looks like varies a bit from browser to browser.

If possible, view your HTML documents on as many different browsers as you can so that you can get a good idea of what your readers may see. You may be surprised at the differences. Take a look at the following screens, which show the same Web page viewed in three different browsers.

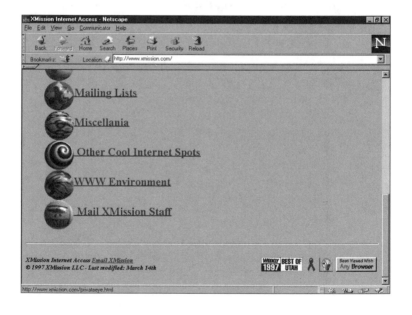

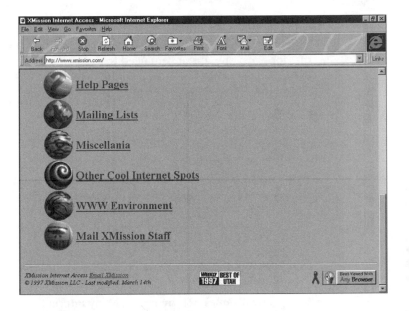

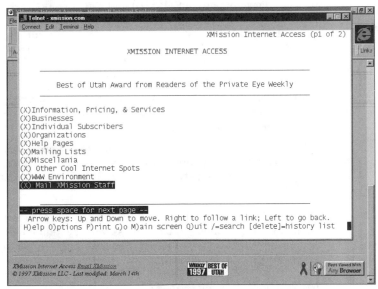

Even such simple pages show differences in font, weight, and size — and, therefore, the amount of information on a page — if viewed in different browsers. The more complex the page designs, the more dramatic these differences can be.

FTP software

If you're planning to publish your HTML documents on the Internet for everyone to see, you need to use *FTP* (*File Transfer Protocol*) software to get your HTML documents and associated files from your computer onto a Web server. Using FTP software is how you officially put your Web pages "out there" (called *publishing* your documents) for all to see. Of course, the trend on the Internet — and, therefore, on the Web — is to make publishing your HTML documents as simple as possible. So publishing may be as easy as the following:

✦ **Using a program that uploads the necessary documents to the server for you, more or less automatically.** Netscape Corporation's Navigator Gold or Composer programs offer a very easy and effective file-upload solution, built right into a WYSIWYG HTML editor to boot. Look around at http:// home.netscape.com for the latest versions. If you're a Windows 95 user, check out Microsoft's Web Publishing Wizard from http://www.microsoft.com.

✦ **Using a traditional FTP program.** Many Internet software packages come with FTP, so if you can currently get on the Web and browse around, you probably already have FTP software. Look for software installed on your computer with FTP in the name (for example, FTP or WS-FTP on Windows — at http://www.ipswitch.com/Products/WS_FTP/ index.html — or Fetch on Macintosh).

✦ **Copying the files into a specific place on a company's local network.** Your network administrator has specific details if this option applies to you.

✦ **Using e-mail to send the documents to a Webmaster.** A *Webmaster* is someone who manages a Web site. Again, your Web server administrator has details if you can use this option.

You don't really know what software or procedures you need to publish your documents until you ask your system administrator or your Internet service provider. *See also* Part VI, "Serving HTML to the World," for more information.

Image editing software

You can (and are likely to choose to) use images in your HTML documents, including logos, photos, drawings, and so on. If you want to use images, you either need a source for ready-made images or need to create the images yourself. Of course, if you don't want to put images in your document, the image-editing software part is optional.

A variety of clip-art libraries are available on the Internet if you'd rather use standard images than create your own. Check out Yahoo! (at `http://www.yahoo.com`) and search for **clip art** to get started.

To create images to use in your HTML document, you need some familiarity with graphics software. Many general purpose drawing or photo editing software packages have options to save files in the correct formats for the Web. Additionally, shareware programs such as Paint Shop Pro (`http://www.jasc.com`) for Windows, GraphicConverter for Macintosh (`http://www.lemkesoft.pinget.de/`), or xv for UNIX (`ftp://ftp.cis.upenn.edu/pub/xv/`) can provide the tools you need.

To find out whether you can create or convert your images, test your favorite drawing or paint program by following these steps:

1. Start your graphics program.

2. Open an image in it (probably by choosing File⇨Open).

3. Choose File⇨Save As.

4. Look for the GIF or JPG options.

If you have these options, you can create the graphics to include in your HTML documents. If you don't find the options you need, you need to either use existing images or check into getting a program that supports the right file formats (using our preceding recommendations, of course).

Or, if you want to use or create fancier graphics, you may need to invest in additional software — probably photo-editing or retouching software, such as Photoshop or Microsoft's Image Composer (the latter bundled as part of the Front Page publishing package).

Publishing HTML Documents

Your HTML documents are not meant to be kept as a secret — you want to *do* something with them. In publishing HTML documents, you have two choices: using a server or not using a server.

Using a server

A *server* is sort of like a waiter or waitress at a restaurant who patiently waits for you to place your order and then brings your meal to you. Likewise, a server waits for people to tell it what information they want and then delivers the information to their computers. You don't even need to leave a tip.

To publish your documents on the Internet or on most intranets, you need access to a server on which you can place HTML documents as well as graphics and related files. Your Internet Service Provider (ISP), for example, probably offers Web space where you can publish your HTML documents (most do). Or, if your ISP doesn't offer a place to publish, many companies provide Web-hosting services for a reasonable fee.

You may also be able to access Web space through your employer's Internet service account. (We do, of course, advise getting permission before putting your personal files on your employer's account.)

After you find a place to publish your HTML documents, you must put them "out there" (on the Web) yourself. As we mentioned, you often do so by transferring your files from your computer to the server by using FTP software. After you transfer a document to the server, that document is generally available to anyone with Web access. See also the section "FTP Software," earlier in this part, for more information about your software options.

Not using a server

If you don't have access to a Web server or don't want the whole world to see your documents, you may have another option for publishing your HTML documents. You can make them available to a select group of people by publishing on a *Local Area Network (LAN)*. A LAN is a network of computers that serves a specific group or organization, such as a company or a university (but doesn't use a Web server as an intranet does).

In publishing on a LAN, your main advantage is that you don't need an Internet connection, Web space, or even a special server (although you can use a Web server on a LAN or intranet, too). And, again, you can publish HTML documents for a group of select people, which comes in handy, say, if you want to publish production schedules or product specifications. You can publish the information strictly for your employees or co-workers without giving others access to that information.

If you're creating HTML documents just for your own satisfaction, you can keep the files on your computer and look at them whenever you want. You keep your documents on your computer while you're testing them anyway, but after finishing your hard work, you probably want to increase their visibility.

We can't go into all of the details about choosing to use a Web server or a LAN. We suggest that you dash off an e-mail to your ISP or corporate network administrator and start asking questions. These administrators answer those questions every day, so you get the latest and greatest answer, tailored to your specific situation.

Understanding All This Stuff

Keep in mind that you can pick up the ins and outs of HTML faster than you think — the language is not as cryptic as it looks. Heck, if we can learn it, you can, too. We do, however, have a few suggestions.

Take one step at a time

As you become familiar with HTML (and even after you have it down cold), we suggest taking one step at a time. Try all the examples that this book provides and even try some of the shortcuts.

You may get frustrated as you're testing your documents. Sometimes you seem to check everything three times — and still nothing works right. Just darn near every time that happens to us (which is just about every day), we check the document again and, sure enough, we find some little, picky, trivial, minute problem that kept everything from working. Patience! Troubleshooting is much easier, too, if you change only one thing at a time — and then make sure that you test thoroughly before moving on.

Be prepared to make a few mistakes, which are likely to be nothing more than typos. Rest assured: You can't do much harm with HTML. You're not going to break your computer, hose up your company's network, or goof up network settings. So have at it!

Borrow ideas

One of the best ways to understand how to use HTML is to look at what other people have done. We certainly don't advocate pilfering ideas from other authors, but you can get a good notion about how different authors create effects in HTML. You can see the tags they use, where they insert something, or the type of background they use just by looking at the HTML document for any given Web page on the Internet. Borrowing ideas — and learning from them — is just a point and click away.

To see the HTML code that people use to create HTML documents on the Internet, open your browser and begin viewing a document. You also need to have your text editor open in case you want to save something. Then follow these steps:

1. Choose View⇨Page Source (Ctrl+U) or View⇨Source from your browser's menu bar (or some similar variation, depending on your browser) to view the original source code used to create the document.

2. If you see something you'd like to copy and save for later (for example, a trick that you hadn't thought of), just use the mouse to highlight the code and press Ctrl+C to copy the text.

If you want to save the entire page, go back to the browser and choose File➪Save As or File➪Save As File from the menu bar (or something similar, depending on your browser).

3. To save the code, paste it into your text editor and choose File➪Save As. You can now examine and reuse this code to your heart's content.

Sometimes instructions in this book refer to menus or menu options that you may not have on your particular setup. Don't worry about these options — just look around for a similar sounding option. Or, if you're really getting close to being stuck, check out the appropriate Dummies book for your computer — *UNIX For Dummies,* 2nd Edition, by John Levine; *Windows 95 For Dummies,* 2nd Edition; *Windows 3.11 For Dummies,* 3rd Edition, both by Andy Rathbone; or *Macintosh For Dummies,* 4th Edition, by David Pogue, all published by IDG Books Worldwide, Inc.

You're probably going to find this process of borrowing ideas or code most useful after you finish this book, but feel free to follow the process at any time to see exactly how your favorite Web pages are constructed. Examining the source code is the easiest way to quickly advance your proficiency.

If examining the source code and trying it out doesn't answer the question of how the author did something, just drop the author an e-mail message (if it's a good page, you probably find a link on the page to send the author an e-mail). Generally, the author of the page is happy to help you or point you to other useful resources.

Part II

Creating an HTML Page

The moment has come — off into the world of HTML we go. *Carpe diem.*

Part II focuses on the formalities (aka the boring stuff) and the fundamentals (aka the fun stuff) of HTML. Knowing how to use these things is necessary for developing good, solid HTML pages — not to mention HTML pages that work. Unfortunately, we can't offer many shortcuts in this section; you'll probably find, however, that after you master HTML, you can whip this stuff out fairly quickly.

Before you start, you may want to review some of the terms introduced in Part I of this book.

If you haven't already, go ahead and open up your text editor and browser so that you can try out the examples we provide. The examples help you begin to put in tags and set up your first HTML document.

In this part . . .

- ✓ Using text and tags
- ✓ Using HTML structure tags
- ✓ Making headings
- ✓ Making paragraphs
- ✓ Emphasizing text
- ✓ Making lists
- ✓ Setting off text

About Text and Tags

HTML documents basically contain the following three things:

✦ Text that you're working with.

✦ Tags that determine document elements such as headings, lists, and paragraphs.

✦ Tags that insert other objects, such as images, sounds, little programs called applets, and movies (although many of these are outside the scope of this book).

You don't generally — at least as you're starting out — need to concern yourself with formatting text or making sure that it looks good. The browser interprets the HTML and does that for you. Instead, you focus on accurately entering the text and tags.

The HTML tags that we describe in this part you use in pairs — one tag goes before the text, and the other tag goes after the text, as in the following example:

```
<TAG>whatever your text is</TAG>
```

✦ The first tag (we call it the *opening tag*) indicates the beginning of a tag that you're applying to some of the text in your document.

✦ The second tag (we call it the *closing tag*) indicates the end of a tag that you're applying.

Everything between the opening and closing tag is affected by the tags.

The initial and closing tags are generally identical, except that the closing tag has a forward slash (/) before the tag name. The tag name is always exactly the same in the opening and closing tags.

Sometimes initial tags also include an attribute, which is just an additional bit of information that further specifies information such as a color, alignment, link address, or text that should appear in place of an image. So, in such a case, an attribute for, say, a background color appears in the initial tag, as follows:

```
<TAG BGCOLOR="#RRGGBB">whatever your text is</TAG>
```

Make sure that you include the forward slash (/) in the closing tag (but don't include the attribute). If you don't include the closing tag, the browser doesn't know that you want to end the style that the tag indicates. And more than likely, the style you applied goes on and on and on until the browser finds a closing tag. We suggest that you go ahead and enter both the initial and closing tags at the same time. That way, you don't forget that essential closing tag.

HTML tags are generally *case-insensitive,* which means that you can type the tags by using either UPPERCASE LETTERS, lowercase letters, or BoTh. We strongly recommend, however, that you type the tags in all caps, because typing the tags in all caps helps you differentiate between the tags and text, particularly after your HTML document becomes pages and pages long.

Make sure that you type the text between the tags so that the text is capitalized just as you want it to appear.

Formatting text

Browsers (*good* ones, at least) disregard all formatting that's not incorporated by using markup tags (such as extra spaces in the HTML document or blank lines that you use to move things down the page). As a result, the extra spaces, lines, or tabs that you put in don't affect your document's appearance.

You, for example, can type your line as follows:

```
<TAG>hill of beans information</TAG>
```

Or you can type the line like this:

```
<TAG>
hill of beans information
</TAG>
```

Or even like the following example:

```
<TAG>
hill
            of
beans

information
</TAG>
```

Any way that you type the tags and text, the result is the same.

If you work with HTML documents frequently, you find that spacing things out and being creative with indentations helps you find your place more easily.

Nesting tags

In many cases, you may want to nest tags inside other tags. *Nesting tags* simply means enclosing tags within tags. By nesting tags, you apply multiple tags to the same bit of text.

Suppose that you want to make text both bold and italic. You can't achieve this effect by using only one tag. Instead, you nest one tag inside the other, as the following example shows:

```
<B><I>more hill of beans information</I></B>
```

See also the section "Emphasizing text," later in this part, for information about the ⟨B⟩ and ⟨I⟩ tags.

Notice that the tag that appears first (in this case, the bold tag) also appears last. If a tag starts first, it ends last. If a tag is right beside the text on the front end, it's right beside the text on the back end as well.

You can also achieve the same effect by switching the order that you start the tags — for example, as in the following line:

```
<I><B>more hill of beans information</B></I>
```

Notice that this example starts with the italic tag and the bold tags are nested within the italic tags. Again, which tag you apply first doesn't matter, as long as you nest them in the same order.

Although most browsers allow you to nest tags and show your document with all the formatting you intend it to have, some older (feeble) browsers don't display this formatting correctly. If you're nesting a ⟨B⟩ and an ⟨I⟩ tag, you may get only one or the other style. These display problems don't happen often, but you need to know what you may occasionally expect. We did mention that you have no guarantees that you can really control what your reader sees, didn't we?

See also Part I, the section "Browsers," for more information about how browsers display things.

Including HTML Structure Tags

Now we move into a group of HTML tags that you use in every HTML document that you create. The first tags in this group are *structure tags* (so named because they define and describe a document's structure). Structure tags are very similar to the key to a map. Although most structure tags do not generally affect the appearance of the document or the information contained within the document, they do help some browsers or HTML-editing programs identify document characteristics.

A couple of these tags also are defined as required parts of a valid HTML document by the people who make the HTML rules (the W3 Consortium, at www.w3.org, in case you're interested). The remaining structure tags are strongly recommended.

Not all browsers or HTML editors require structure tags to open and display the HTML document. Because you don't know the types of browsers that your users may have, however, we also recommend that you include these tags in every HTML document you create. You may create a cool document that's useless if your user can't access it. If you don't want to put structure tags in all the time, make sure that you put them in your resumé or in anything else important.

For most HTML documents, you use five structure tags, which we list in the following table and describe in the following sections.

HTML Structure Tag	Purpose	Use in Pairs?
`<!DOCTYPE HTML PUBLIC "-//W3C//DTD HTML 3.2 Final//EN">`	Identifies document as an HTML document and specifies HTML version. Mandatory in all HTML documents.	No
`<HTML>...</HTML>`	Defines the document as an HTML document.	Yes
`<HEAD>...</HEAD>`	Includes introductory information about the document.	Yes
`<TITLE>...</TITLE>`	Indicates the document title. Mandatory in all HTML documents.	Yes
`<BODY>...</BODY>`	Encloses all elements within the main portion of the document.	Yes

Note: Before you begin, make sure that you have your browser and text editor open.

The !DOCTYPE tag

The !DOCTYPE tag is a nonpaired tag that identifies the document as an HTML document and appears at the top of every HTML document. Specifically, this tag notes that the document conforms to specific HTML standards — generally, to the final HTML Version 3.2 standards. Pretty comprehensive for such a cryptic line of stuff, huh? If you use HTML editing programs, they probably put the !DOCTYPE tag in automatically. If they don't, however, make sure that you type the !DOCTYPE tag in at the top of all your documents. (If you don't, nothing will break and the world won't end. But better safe than sorry, right?)

Suppose that you want to create an HTML document about making a water balloon. Enter the !DOCTYPE tag as follows:

```
<!DOCTYPE HTML PUBLIC "-//W3C//DTD HTML 3.2
    Final//EN">
```

The <HTML> tag

The <HTML> tag encloses everything except the !DOCTYPE tag in every document. This tag, as the name indicates, defines that HTML is used to create the document. If you don't specify HTML, the browser may not read the tags as tags. Instead, the browser may read the tags as text, in which case, the document looks pretty much as it does in the text editor. In short, your document looks like a traffic accident — with stuff strewn everywhere and with at least one panicked person (that's you, the person who caused the accident).

Taking the water balloon page, enter the <HTML> tags at the beginning and end of the document, as shown in the following example:

```
<!DOCTYPE HTML PUBLIC "-//W3C//DTD HTML 3.2
    Final//EN">
<HTML>
. . .all the stuff about making water balloons will
go here eventually. . .
</HTML>
```

The <HEAD> and <TITLE> tags

The <HEAD> tag is part of what many browsers use to identify or reference the document. Without this tag, some browsers can't open and display the document for the reader correctly. For many HTML developers, the <HEAD> tag seems completely useless. Keep in mind that, although this tag doesn't have a visible application for creating an HTML document, it does have a technical application.

The <TITLE> tag — which the HTML specification requires — simply applies a title of your choice to the document. Make your title as descriptive as you can so that people can find or identify your documents more easily on the Internet.

Taking the water balloon document one more step, add the <HEAD> and <TITLE> tags as shown in the following example:

```
<!DOCTYPE HTML PUBLIC "-//W3C//DTD HTML 3.2
    Final//EN">
<HTML>
<HEAD><TITLE>Making Effective Water Balloons
    </TITLE>
</HEAD>
. . .all the stuff about making water balloons. . .
</HTML>
```

Notice that the <HEAD> and <TITLE> tags appear immediately after the initial <HTML> tag.

The *<BODY>* tag

The <BODY> tag indicates that all information contained within the initial and closing tags is part of the document body, not part of the rest of the document, as are the other tags we've introduced. Without this tag, the browser doesn't know that the information should appear as part of the document. Everything you want people to see must be contained between the <BODY> and </BODY> tags.

You place the <BODY> tag at the very beginning of the information that you want to put into your HTML document. Technically, all other tags that you use are nested between the <BODY> and </BODY> tags.

You actually begin the water balloon project by adding the <BODY> tags, as follows:

```
<!DOCTYPE HTML PUBLIC "-//W3C//DTD HTML 3.2
    Final//EN">
<HTML>
<HEAD><TITLE>Making Effective Water Balloons
    </TITLE>
</HEAD>
<BODY>
. . .all the stuff about making water balloons. . .
</BODY>
</HTML>
```

And that's all, folks! Those are the main structure tags that you use to create all your HTML documents.

See also Appendix A for more structure tags that you may use on occasion. Additionally, some other tags may be automatically inserted into your HTML documents by editor or converter programs. You'll probably get to the point that you recognize these tags, but you won't have to use them unless you really want to.

Avoid some future trouble now by saving the basic HTML file (with the head, title, and body tags) under some easy-to-remember name. If you just reuse the file, you don't need to type those stinking tags again.

Using Basic HTML Tags

Basic HTML tags are the ones that enable you to create simple, yet functional effects in your HTML documents. This section describes the tags necessary for making headings, paragraphs, and lists and for emphasizing and setting off text. These tags don't produce the flashiest of HTML documents; they do, however, produce effects that you use in most of, if not all, your HTML documents.

You're simply applying tags to text — precisely what the text looks like to your readers depends on the browser they use, the computer system they use, and the specific settings of their system. Again, you don't necessarily have direct control over what the readers actually see. That's just the way HTML works. Go ahead and try out the examples as you read through the information.

Note: Before you begin, make sure that you have your browser and text editor open.

Making headings

HTML offers you six choices in headings, labeled as ⟨H1⟩ through ⟨H6⟩. ⟨H1⟩ is the largest and boldest of the headings, and ⟨H6⟩ is the smallest and least bold one. You can use these headings to show a hierarchy of information (such as the headings in this book).

HTML Tag	Effect	Use in Pairs?
⟨H1⟩. . .⟨/H1⟩	Heading 1	Yes
⟨H2⟩. . .⟨/H2⟩	Heading 2	Yes
⟨H3⟩. . .⟨/H3⟩	Heading 3	Yes
⟨H4⟩. . .⟨/H4⟩	Heading 4	Yes
⟨H5⟩. . .⟨/H5⟩	Heading 5	Yes
⟨H6⟩. . .⟨/H6⟩	Heading 6	Yes

The heading tags go in pairs — for example, ⟨H1⟩. . .⟨/H1⟩. And as with all other paired tags, the text that you want to include goes between the tags. These headings look somewhat like the example shown in the following figure, as displayed in a browser.

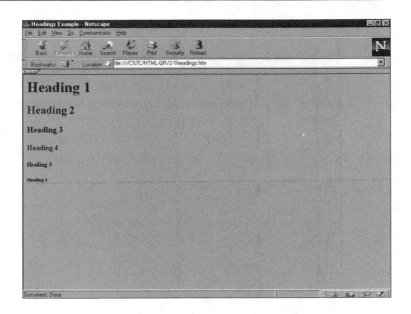

Many people have discovered that the ⟨H6⟩ tags are really small — very, very small — and tend to use ⟨H6⟩ tags to create small text on their pages. Unfortunately, these same people have also discovered that automatically generated tables of contents or indexes of their pages include their very small copyright notices and disclaimers right up there with the important heading stuff. Hmmm. Be careful to use heading tags only as they're intended — for headings!

One of the first things you do is to put a heading in your document. In most cases, the first heading — the ⟨H1⟩ heading — is the name of your document — for example, "Making Effective Water Balloons." You enter the tags and text as shown in the following example:

```
<H1>Making Effective Water Balloons</H1>
```

Suppose that you want to use other headings within your document. You enter these lower-level headings the same way, as the following example demonstrates:

```
<H1>Making Effective Water Balloons</H1>
<H2>Mission Name:Cat Splats</H2>
<H3>Materials Used to Create Cat Splats</H3>
<H3>Methods Used in Cat Splat Mission</H3>
<H2>Timing the Cat Splat</H2>
<H2>Evaluating the Success of the Cat Splat Mission
    </H2>
```

The following figure shows how this code looks in a Web browser.

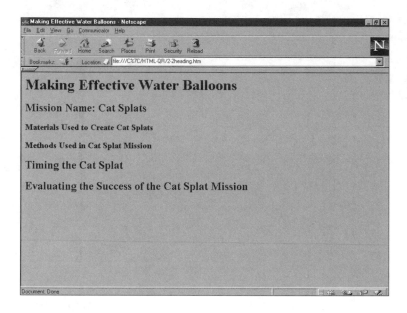

Making paragraphs

By using HTML, you can separate information into paragraphs. The HTML paragraph tag, `<P>`, indicates the beginning and the end of a paragraph of text, respectively, as the following table shows.

HTML Tag	Effect	Use in Pairs?
`<P>. . .</P>`	Indicates a paragraph.	`</P>` is optional.

Suppose that you want to start adding information to the "Making Effective Water Balloons" document. All you do is build on your structure tags or existing information, as the following example shows:

```
<!DOCTYPE HTML PUBLIC "-//W3C//DTD HTML 3.2
    Final//EN">
<HTML>
<HEAD><TITLE>Making Effective Water Balloons
    </TITLE>
</HEAD>
<BODY>
<H1>Making Effective Water Balloons</H1>
<P>
Making a water balloon is easy . . . but making
effective water balloons takes time and patience.
```

```
The result is a water balloon that does not break
in your hand, offers maximum splashing power, and
requires virtually no post-splat clean up.
</P>
</BODY>
</HTML>
```

The following figure shows the result of this HTML code in a Web browser.

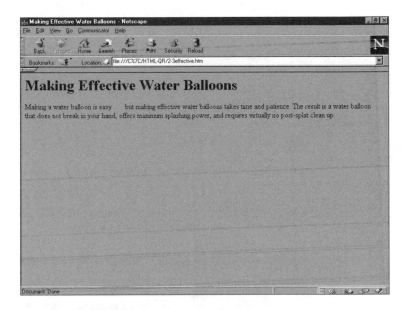

Emphasizing text

After you write something, you may want to make some of the words within the text stand out. HTML offers several options for doing this, including emphasizing text and adding bold and italic to text. The following table describes some of these options.

HTML Tag	Effect	Use in Pairs?
`<EM>. . .</EM>`	Adds emphasis (usually appears as italic).	Yes
`<STRONG>. . .</STRONG>`	Adds strong emphasis (usually appears as bold).	Yes
`<B>. . .</B>`	Adds boldface.	Yes
`<I>. . .</I>`	Adds italics.	Yes

To emphasize the text in the paragraph on making effective water balloons, you can add emphasis to the word "easy" and strong emphasis to the word "effective." You can also add boldface to "break" and italics to "maximum splashing power." The following example demonstrates the use of these tags:

```
<!DOCTYPE HTML PUBLIC "-//W3C//DTD HTML 3.2
    Final//EN">
<HTML>
<HEAD><TITLE>Making Effective Water Balloons
    </TITLE>
</HEAD>
<BODY>
<H1>Making Effective Water Balloons</H1>
<P>
Making water balloons is <EM>easy</EM> . . . but
making <STRONG>effective</STRONG> water balloons
takes time and patience. The result is a water
balloon that does not <B>break</B> in your hand,
offers <I>maximum splashing power</I>, and requires
virtually no post splat clean up.
</P>
</BODY>
</HTML>
```

Notice that the tags are positioned around the word or words that you want to emphasize. The following figure shows how these codes change the appearance of the Web page.

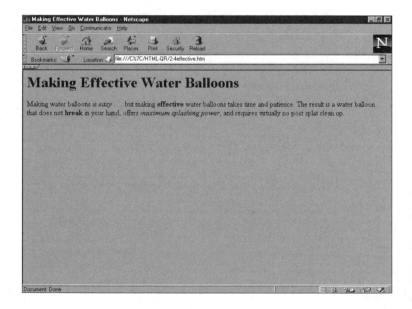

You can also add more than one kind of emphasis to a word. Suppose that you want to add both ⟨I⟩ and ⟨B⟩ to the word "easy." You do so as follows:

```
<P>
Making a water balloon is <I><B>easy</B></I>.
</P>
```

In this case, the ⟨B⟩ tags are nested inside the ⟨I⟩ tags. You can also nest the ⟨I⟩ tags inside the ⟨B⟩ tags. The order in which you nest the tags doesn't matter.

If you don't want the punctuation to appear emphasized, make sure that you place it outside the emphasis tags, as shown in the preceding example.

If possible, we recommend that you use *logical* formatting tags — ⟨EM⟩, ⟨STRONG⟩ — rather than the *physical* ones — ⟨B⟩, ⟨I⟩. Some people may have browsers that cannot display italics or boldface. If you tell the browser to emphasize the text in any way possible (logical formatting), one browser may boldface the text, while others may underline the text or show it in reverse video. If you just tell the browser to put something in boldface (physical formatting), but it can't, the browser ignores you, and the key phrase remains ⟨EM⟩unemphasized⟨/EM⟩.

Making lists

Often you may want to provide information in lists rather than in paragraphs. Providing information in lists is especially valuable in HTML documents, because lists allow the reader to gather information quickly without needing to wade through paragraphs of text. And for you, the writer, making lists is an easy way to help organize your information and provide easy links to other pages. (*See also* Part III for more information about links.)

Making lists is a two-part process:

First, you must add a pair of tags to specify that the information is to appear in a list. You can specify, for example, an *ordered* (or numbered) list, ⟨OL⟩...⟨/OL⟩; or an *unordered* (or bulleted) list, ⟨UL⟩...⟨/UL⟩. You use ordered lists if you want to list things that need to go in a specific order, such as instructions. You use unordered lists if you just want to make a list of things, such as ingredients for water balloons.

Second, you must specify each line of the list, called line items, ⟨LI⟩. Just put the ⟨LI⟩ tag at the beginning of each line, where you want the number or bullet to be. No closing tag is required here.

Make sure that you use lists whenever possible. After a few hours of cruising around HTML pages, readers' eyes get pretty buggy, and they kinda' gloss over several paragraphs in a row. Readers still, however, read the lists. Lists are the "music-video/short-attention-span" approach to organizing information, as opposed to the "extended-essay" approach.

The following table shows the tags you use to create lists.

HTML Tag	Effect	Use in Pairs?
`<LI>`	Identifies each item in a list.	No
`<OL>. . .</OL>`	Specifies ordered (numbered) lists.	Yes
`<UL>. . .</UL>`	Specifies unordered (bulleted) lists.	Yes

To add an unordered (bulleted) list of materials to the "Making Effective Water Balloons" page, perform the following steps:

1. Add opening and closing `<UL>` tags where you want the list to appear, as shown in the following example:

```
<!DOCTYPE HTML PUBLIC "-//W3C//DTD HTML 3.2
    Final//EN">
<HTML>
<HEAD><TITLE>Making Effective Water Balloons
    </TITLE>
</HEAD>
<BODY>
<H1>Making Effective Water Balloons</H1>
<P>
Making water balloons is <EM>easy</EM> . . .
but making <B>effective</B> water balloons
takes time and patience. The result is a water
balloon that does not break in your hand,
offers <I>maximum splashing power</I>, and
requires virtually no post-splat clean up.
</P>
<H2>Materials Needed</H2>
<UL>
</UL>
</BODY>
</HTML>
```

2. Add `<LI>` tags for each item, along with the text for the item, as follows:

```
<UL>
<LI>Water
<LI>Big, big balloon
<LI>Balloon ties (optional)
<LI>Second-story window
<LI>Target below window
</UL>
```

The following figure shows the results of adding these tags and text.

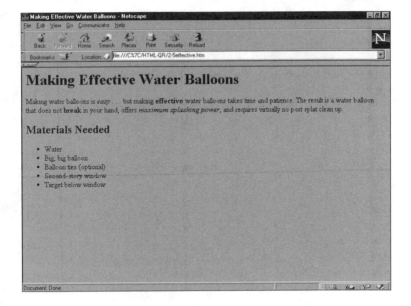

Notice that the list tags don't have <P> tags around them. If you have a list you don't need a <P>.

To add an ordered list of instructions on how to make effective water balloons, you use the <OL> tags, as follows:

1. Add opening and closing <OL> tags where the list appears, as in the following example.

```
<H2>Instructions</H2>
<OL>
</OL>
```

2. Add <LI> tags and text for each item, as follows:

```
<H2>Instructions</H2>
<OL>
<LI>Fill balloon with water.
<LI>Tie balloon using a tie or by making a
    knot.
<LI>Go to second-story window.
<LI>Aim at spot below window.
<LI>Drop balloon.
</OL>
```

These examples appear as shown in the following figure.

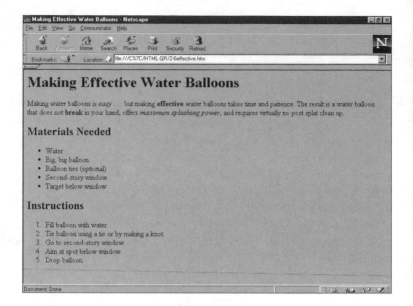

TIP

You can add attributes (extra information) to your list tags to control what the bullets look like, what kind of numbers (Roman, capital letters, regular Arabic numbers, and so on) appear, and what the starting number is for sequential lists. See Appendix A for the specific attributes.

Setting off text

Occasionally, you need to set off information from the rest of the text. HTML enables you to set off text by using a number of body markup tags (listed comprehensively in Appendix A, under the heading "Body Markup"). These tags are all used in a very similar fashion, so after you've mastered one set, you're all set to use the rest of them as well.

You may, for example, have a really neat quotation to include in your page. Because quotations are often visibly different from the rest of the text (by virtue of indents on both sides), you use a different tag to identify the quote — the <BLOCKQUOTE>. . . </BLOCKQUOTE> tags, to be specific. This pair of tags makes the text look just like the body text but with an increased amount of white space in both margins. The following table presents this tag's pertinent information.

HTML Tag	Effect	Use in Pairs?
`<BLOCKQUOTE>`. . . `</BLOCKQUOTE>`	Increases margins on both sides.	Yes

We can include the quotation by using the `<BLOCKQUOTE>` tags in the water balloons document, as shown in the following example:

```
<!DOCTYPE HTML PUBLIC "-//W3C//DTD HTML 3.2
    Final//EN">
<HTML>
<HEAD><TITLE>Making Effective Water Balloons
    </TITLE>
</HEAD>
<BODY>
<H1>Making Effective Water Balloons</H1>
<P>
Making water balloons is <EM>easy</EM> . . . but
making <B>effective</B> water balloons takes time
and patience. The result is a water balloon that
does not break in your hand, offers <I>maximum
splashing power</I>, and requires virtually no
post-splat clean up.
</P>
<H2>Instructions</H2>
<OL>
<LI>Fill balloon with water.
<LI>Tie balloon using tie or by making a knot.
<LI>Go to second-story window.
<LI>Aim at spot below window.
<LI>Drop balloon.
</OL>
<H2>Additional Ponderings . . . </H2>
<P>After using these instructions, you might hear
    comments like the following one.</P>
<BLOCKQUOTE>
Although that was very cold, I do say that it was
quite refreshing. As a matter of fact, I can't
remember the last time I was so incredibly re-
freshed. And wet.
</BLOCKQUOTE>
<P>Mighty amusing, isn't it?</P>
</BODY>
</HTML>
```

The following figure shows this addition in a Web browser.

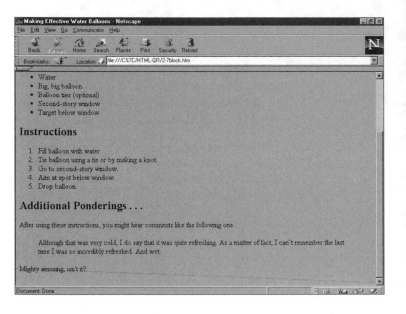

- Water
- Big, big balloon
- Balloon ties (optional)
- Second-story window
- Target below window

Instructions

1. Fill balloon with water.
2. Tie balloon using a tie or by making a knot.
3. Go to second-story window.
4. Aim at spot below window.
5. Drop balloon.

Additional Ponderings . . .

After using these instructions, you might hear comments like the following one.

Although that was very cold, I do say that it was quite refreshing. As a matter of fact, I can't remember the last time I was so incredibly refreshed. And wet.

Mighty amusing, isn't it?.

Part III

Spinning Your HTML Web

In this part, you see how to add anchors and links to your HTML documents. Anchors and links allow your readers to jump from place to place within your document or to other documents and files. So get ready for the wild Web of HTML.

You apply lots of tags in this section, so if initial tags, closing tags, and phrases such as "applying the markup tags to your document" are unfamiliar, you may want to go back to Part II for more information about HTML basics.

In this part . . .

- ✔ Figuring out links
- ✔ Figuring out URLs
- ✔ Figuring out anchors
- ✔ Linking to documents within your own site
- ✔ Linking to documents out on the Web
- ✔ Linking to other material on the Web
- ✔ Linking to specific places with HTML documents

About Links

In creating HTML documents, you're creating documents that users can read by *linking* from topic to topic — that is, jumping from page to page and from topic to topic instead of moving linearly, as in a novel. *Links* (or *hyperlinks* or *hot spots*) are places that users can select to access other topics, documents, or *Web sites* (collection of HTML documents).

As you build your HTML documents, think about how you want your documents to link together. As a rule, you should create several short HTML documents rather than one long document. Short documents are easier for your readers to follow and are, therefore, more likely to be read. You can then link these shorter documents into a single cohesive set of documents (that is, a Web site).

If you expect to be revising and updating the information frequently, however, or if your readers are intended to print out the documents and refer to them on hard copy (tree killer!), you should use fewer, but longer, documents to reduce your headaches as well as those of your readers.

To create a link (or *anchor*), you need the following two things:

✦ A *URL* (or *U*niform *R*esource *L*ocator), which is just an address on the Web.

✦ An *anchor tag,* which marks the link in a Web page.

About URLs

A *URL* (pronounced You-Are-Ell), or *Uniform Resource Locator,* is a fancy way of saying an address for information on the Internet. If you hear URL, just think "address" or "location." URLs differ based on how specific you need to be.

URLs can be *absolute* (complete) or *relative* (partial), as described in the following list:

✦ If you're creating a document that you want to publish on the Internet, you indicate the absolute URL so that anyone in the world using the Internet can find the page.

✦ If you're creating links to other files within the same folder, you can include only a relative URL, because you're already in the same directory (or folder) as the file to which you're linking.

See also "Absolute and Relative URLs," later in this part.

All HTML documents can use URLs to link to other information. URLs, in turn, can point to many different things, such as HTML documents, other sites on the Internet, or even images and sound files.

URLs are *case-sensitive*. On some computers, typing a filename such as Kitten.html is very different from typing kitten.html. If you create a filename that uses special capitalization (instead of, say, using all lowercase characters), you must use this same capitalization the same way every time you link to the document.

Anatomy of URLs

If you're not used to them, URLs can be pretty odd looking. Each part of a URL has a built-in specific meaning, however, much like each part of your home address. The street address "12 Fritter Lane, Apartment G, Santa Clara, CA 95051," for example, provides a postal carrier with essential and complete information — the specific apartment in a specific building on a specific street in a specific town in a specific state in a specific Zip code.

URLs work the same way by providing a browser with all the parts it needs to locate information. A URL consists of the *protocol indicator,* the *hostname,* and the *directory name* and/or *filename.* The following (fictitious) URL is an example of an absolute URL:

http://cat.feline.org/fur/fuzzy.html

Here's a description of each URL part:

✦ The http:// portion (the *protocol indicator*) tells the server how to send the information. The protocol indicator is the standard used by Web servers and browsers that lets them talk to each other. If you're creating HTML documents, people point to them by using http:// as the protocol indicator.

See also Part I and Part VI for more information about servers.

✦ The cat.feline.org portion (the *hostname*) specifies a computer on the Internet. If you publish an HTML document, you're placing it on a computer that "serves" the document to anyone who knows the correct URL. This computer has an address that's common to all documents that it stores. The server thus "hosts" all these documents and makes them accessible to users.

To discover the hostname of the server on which you place your files, check with your system administrator.

✦ The `fur` portion is the directory name. You may not need to show a directory name, or you may have several that represent directories inside directories (or folders inside folders). If you have an account with an Internet Service Provider, your directory name may also begin with a ~ and your user name, yielding something such as `http://cat.feline.org/` `~lucy/`, assuming, of course, that `lucy` is the account name.

✦ The `fuzzy.html` portion is the name of the file that's located on the host computer. Sometimes you don't need to provide a filename — the server simply gives out the default file in the directory. The default filenames are usually one of three: `index.html`, `default.html`, or `homepage.html`, depending on which kind of Web server the files are located. The filename is like many other files; it contains a name (`fuzzy`) and an extension (`.html`).

Sometimes URLs have a hostname with a port number at the end (for example, `cat.feline.org:80`). This number gives the server more precise information about the URL. If you see a URL with a number, just leave the number on the URL. If you don't see a number, don't worry about it.

Try to avoid creating directory names or filenames with spaces or other unusual characters. Stay with letters (uppercase and lowercase), numbers, underscores (_), periods (.), or plus signs (+). Some servers have problems with odd characters. And if you do use any capitalization in your filenames, you must also use the same capitalization in any links pointing to those files, because some servers require consistent capitalization. Our advice? Stay away from capitalization — just use lowercase letters.

Absolute and Relative URLs

As we mention earlier in this part, links in Web pages use two different types of URLs: *absolute URLs* and *relative URLs*. Each of these types of URLs has a specific purpose and uses specific components, as the following list describes:

✦ *Absolute URLs* give the full address of something on the Internet. They include the protocol indicator, hostname, and directory name/filenames. You use absolute URLs to indicate any location on the Internet.

Keep in mind that pointing people to Internet locations requires as much information as you can provide, just as you'd provide very detailed information to an out-of-town friend who's driving to your apartment. You'd provide, for example, the state, city, building number, and apartment number (unless, of course, you want that friend to get lost).

Similarly, you need to provide as complete a URL as possible so that people around the world can find your Web site.

✦ *Relative URLs* don't contain a complete address, but they can still provide all the information you need to link to other documents. A relative URL usually contains only the last part of the absolute URL — the directory name (possibly) and the filename. You use relative URLs to link to locations within the same folder or same group of folders.

To go back to that postal address analogy, if you're giving a local friend directions to your apartment, you'd probably just provide the street address, building, and apartment. The city and state are implicit. In the same way, a relative URL implies the missing information based on the location of the file containing the relative URL. The browser infers the missing information from the location of the document containing the link.

A relative URL that starts with a slash (/) is a server-relative URL — you can just add the name of the server to the beginning of the URL, and you get the complete URL. A relative URL that doesn't start with a slash may not be relative to the server, so adding the server name doesn't produce a complete URL, because the browser may need more information about the file location.

Huh? How about an example: Suppose that, in the http://cat.feline.org/fur/fuzzy.html document, you want to link users to more information within the same folder (say, information about kittens). Instead of typing the entire URL again, plus kitten.html, you use kitten.html for the URL in the current document. The computer understands that, if you include an incomplete URL in a link, the rest of the information is derived from the location of the file from which you're linking.

Also, within the fuzzy.html document, you may have pointers to other documents using partial URLs on the same server — for example, /colors/calico.html and /colors/tortoiseshell.html. The calico.html and tortoiseshell.html files are located within the colors directory. These files are server-relative — they all have the same server. So you can add http://cat.feline.org to the beginning and have an accurate URL.

Of course, you need the absolute URL only if you're linking from another location or if you're entering the URL directly in your browser. If you're linking from another document located on the same server, you can just use the relative URL in your document.

Relative URLs are great for weaving a whole web of HTML documents with all kinds of interconnections. You can put your documents on a server or give them to someone else for installation on another computer, and the links among the documents continue to work. As a matter of fact, unless you need to use an absolute URL (to point to an entirely different Internet site, for example), don't. Relative URLs are just more practical.

Check out the following figure, which shows how absolute URLs and relative URLs work.

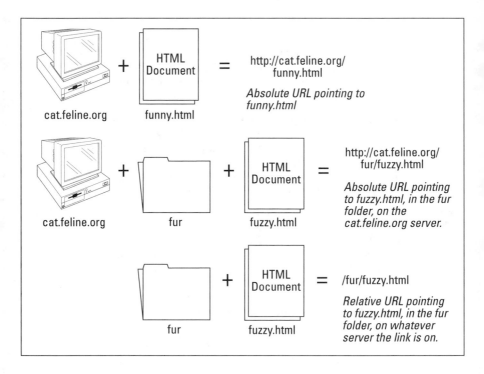

About Anchors

The linking process begins with *anchors;* this term is just a fancy way of saying links. (We call them anchors because the tag is ⟨A⟩.)

Anchor tags are generally used with one of the following two attributes:

✦ HREF allows users to jump from one bit of information to another — either to material within the same Web site or to other material out on the Internet. These tags create the hyperlinks.

✦ NAME labels a spot within a document. That spot can then be
part of a URL so that readers can jump directly to it. The NAME
anchor is useful in long documents that users must otherwise
scroll through. As a result, users can jump to specific information and don't need to wade through pages of material.

HTML Markup (attributes in italics)	Effect	Use in Pairs?
`<A>. . .</A>`	Marks anchor.	Yes
`HREF=". . ."`	Indicates where to jump.	No
`NAME=". . ."`	Identifies an internal label.	No

Making Your First Links

Links are the connections to other material within or among HTML
documents. Links are visible as (generally blue) text that you
select as you're surfing the Web. (After you've linked to a document, the link then appears in a different color to indicate that
you've already been there.) The next three sections show you how
to link to other documents within your site, link to HTML documents "out there" on the Web, and link to other information on the
Internet. For now, you work with the HREF attribute.

Linking to documents within your site

Here you start with plain text and build your first hypertext link.
We recommend that you work with two, preferably small, HTML
documents so that you can link from one to the other and back
again. Practicing linking is much more difficult if you work with
just one document.

Note: Before beginning the example in this section, open your text
editor and browser. While trying these examples, you should also
have available a basic HTML document, such as the following:

```
<!DOCTYPE HTML PUBLIC "-//W3C//DTD HTML 3.2
    Final//EN">
<HTML><HEAD><TITLE>Cats</TITLE></HEAD>
<BODY>

</BODY>
</HTML>
```

Now follow these steps:

1. Enter **Cats are funny** between the <BODY> tags, as the
following example shows:

```
<BODY>
Cats are funny.
</BODY>
```

2. Apply the anchor tags to `funny`, as follows, to make that word the anchor (the part that your readers click to link to something else):

```
Cats are <A>funny</A>.
```

3. Add an attribute (`HREF=`, in this case) to link to another document, as follows:

```
Cats are <A HREF="funny.html">funny</A>.
```

`HREF=` is the attribute that specifies which document appears after your readers click the anchor. And `funny.html` is the name of the document to which you are linking.

In this case, `funny.html` is a file in the same directory or folder as the document that you're building.

If you want to link the same bit of text to a file within a new folder, just add the necessary folder information, as follows:

```
Cats are <A HREF="newfolder/funny.html">funny</A>.
```

Notice the slash. Its function is to separate the directory or folder name and the filename. The slash is a required element of a pathname.

To link the same bit of text to a file in a folder somewhere else on the server, you can make a server-relative URL by adding a slash and a folder name, as follows:

```
Cats are <A HREF="/folderonserver/funny.html">
   funny</A>.
```

If you create one of these URLs, you must check to make sure that it really *is* a server-relative URL. If you can't add the server name to the beginning and make it work, don't put a slash at the beginning of the relative URL.

Linking to pages out on the Web

To create links to other documents on the Internet, follow the same procedure as with other links, but include the complete URL in the `HREF` attribute.

To make a link from the word *cats* to a completely different address, use the following example, starting with the following basic HTML document.

Note: Before beginning, open your text editor and browser.

```
<!DOCTYPE HTML PUBLIC "-//W3C//DTD HTML 3.2
    Final//EN">
<HTML><HEAD><TITLE>Cats</TITLE></HEAD>
<BODY>

</BODY>
</HTML>
```

Use the following steps to add a link to a document at another location:

1. Type **Cats are funny** between the `<BODY>` tags, as follows:

```
<BODY>
Cats are funny.
</BODY>
```

2. Add the following anchor tags:

```
<A>Cats</A> are funny.
```

3. Add the `HREF` attribute to link to a sample (fictitious) Web site about cats, as follows:

```
<A HREF="http://cats.com/home.html">Cats</A>
    are funny.
```

You can also link to files from a regular `http://` type address. If, for example, you have a Word document that you want people to be able to download from your Web site, you could put in a link such as the following:

```
<A HREF="catjokes.doc">Download original cat
    stories here</A>.
```

Or you could use an absolute URL, as follows:

```
<A HREF="http://cat.feline.org/furry/
    catjokes.doc">Download original cat stories
    here</A>.
```

Then all you need to do is upload the `catjokes.doc` file to the server at the same time that you upload your HTML document to the server.

As you're making anchors, try to avoid using "Click here." By the time they see your page, your readers have probably figured out that they need to click links to go from one place to another.

Linking to other stuff on the Internet

Just as you can link to HTML documents or images or files on the Internet by including the right URL, you can also link to other types of information (such as discussion groups or file archives) on the Internet. All kinds of other *protocols* (the language that computers use to transfer information) are in use. The following table describes some of these protocols.

Protocol	URL	Always Acceptable?
HTTP	`http://`	Yes
FTP	`ftp://`	Yes
Gopher	`gopher://`	Yes
News (NNTP)	`news:`	No
Mail	`mailto:`	No
Telnet	`telnet://`	No
File	`file://` or `file:///`	Yes
Wais	`wais://`	No

If you see or hear of neat material on the Internet that's available through an *FTP site* (a source for data on the Internet), you can link that material into your document.

See also Part I for information about FTP (File Transfer Protocol).

Some of the less-often-used URLs can cause problems, depending on the browser your readers are using and how the browser is set up. If you suspect that they're using old browsers or that they haven't configured their browsers completely (or correctly), we recommend staying away from the URLs that aren't "always acceptable," as described in the preceding table.

To use one of the other listed protocol indicators, substitute it for the `http://` that you normally use. Your URL may, for example, start with `gopher://` rather than `http://`.

Suppose that your best friend found a collection of cat jokes at an FTP site on the Internet. You can simply copy the URL from your friend. The URL may look something like `ftp://humor.central.org/jokes/animals/cats.zip`. You can put that URL into your document as shown in the following example.

Note: Before beginning the example in this section, open your text editor and browser and start with a basic HTML document such as the following example.

```
<!DOCTYPE HTML PUBLIC "-//W3C//DTD HTML 3.2
    Final//EN">
<HTML><HEAD><TITLE>Cats</TITLE></HEAD>
<BODY>

</BODY>
</HTML>
```

Use these steps to add the link to your document:

1. Type **A collection of cat jokes is good to have** between the `<BODY>` tags, as follows:

```
<BODY>
A collection of cat jokes is good to have.
</BODY>
```

2. Add the following anchor tags:

```
A collection of <A>cat jokes</A> is good to
have.
```

3. Add the `HREF` attribute to link to the file, as follows:

```
A collection of <A HREF="ftp://humor.
central.org/jokes/animals/cats.zip">cat
jokes</A> is good to have.
```

The best way to get URLs into your documents is to follow these steps:

1. Use the *location line* in your Web browser.

(The location line is the line — at the top — that starts with `http://`.)

2. Click the location line of your browser while you're cruising the Internet and find a neat site.

3. Highlight the address and copy it by using the keystroke command that you normally use on your system — probably Ctrl+C.

4. Go back to your editing program and paste in the URL wherever you want it — probably by pressing Ctrl+V.

This step greatly reduces the risk of typos.

As you're putting links into your Web pages, be careful about linking to `news:` URLs. Different *news servers* (sources for Usenet News on the Internet) offer access to varying groups. You may link to your favorite group, but many users may not be able to get to it because their news servers don't carry that particular group.

Usenet News is a huge collection of discussion groups. For more information about Usenet News, see *The Internet For Dummies,* 4th Edition, by John R. Levine, Carol Baroudi, and Margaret Levine Young (published by IDG Books Worldwide, Inc.).

Generally, you should also link to a specific news group rather than to a specific article. A specific article is likely to cease to exist at some point, in which case your link no longer works.

Making Links Within Documents

Making links to places within an HTML document requires a little more work than does creating the links to other documents that we've been talking about. On regular links to other documents or to documents on other servers, you just point to a computer and a file. If you're going to point to a place *within a document* that you're creating, however, you must also identify the targets to which you intend to link.

Making Internal Links

An *internal link* points to a specific location within a document. Internal links work really well if you have a long HTML document that really doesn't lend itself to being split into different files. If you're dealing with one of these long documents, you can use internal links to point from one place to another within the same document. As a result, readers don't need to scroll through pages of information; they can just link to a place (defined by a special anchor) within the document.

Within the `kitten.html` file, you may have a long list of favorite kitten names along with a description of the names' origins. You can enable readers to jump right to the "W" names without needing to scroll through the "A" through "V" names. The following URL points directly to the "w" anchor within the `kitten.html` file:

`kitten.html#w`

The relative URL could also possibly be written as follows:

`fur/kitten.html#w`

or

`/fur/kitten.html#w`

Or you could write the address as the following absolute URL:

`http://cat.feline.org/fur/kitten.html#w`

Marking internal targets

Developing anchors to permit links to points within a document is very similar to creating the links themselves. You use the `NAME=` attribute that we mention in the preceding section. These targets are called *name anchors,* or *internal targets.*

(In the preceding example, the author of `kitten.html` inserted name anchors for all 26 A–Z headings, just so that you can link to them.)

For the following example, imagine that you have a heading within your document called "Funny Cats I've Known."

Note: Before beginning, open your text editor and browser. You should also have a basic HTML document such as the following one available while you try these examples:

```
<!DOCTYPE HTML PUBLIC "-//W3C//DTD HTML 3.2
    Final//EN">
<HTML><HEAD><TITLE>Cats</TITLE></HEAD>
<BODY>
<H2>Funny Cats I've Known</H2>
General information about the cats would be here.
</BODY>
</HTML>
```

Now follow these steps to include the anchor:

1. Include an anchor, as follows:

```
<H2><A>Funny</A> Cats I've Known</H2>
```

2. Insert the NAME= attribute, as follows:

```
<H2><A NAME="funny">Funny</A> Cats I've Known
    </H2>
```

This anchor doesn't show up in the browser view of your document, but you know it's there.

If you're preparing HTML documents that someone may use for reference or to which other people may be interested in linking their pages, we suggest inserting some logical NAME= anchors. Even if you don't think you can use them, you'll find that putting them in while you're creating your page is easier than putting them in later.

If you want to link directly to the funny cats section of your document from within the same document, you can include a link to #funny, as follows:

```
<A HREF="#funny">Funny cats</A> are here.
```

The #funny anchor to which you want to link, for example, may be in the cats.html file on the server called cat.feline.org. You just create a URL that looks as follows:

```
http://cat.feline.org/cats.html#funny
```

Your friends and admirers can then set up links to your funny cats section:

```
Boy, you know, those <A HREF="http://
cat.feline.org/cats.html#funny">funny cats
</A> are something else.
```

Using Images in Your Web Pages

Part IV focuses on using images in your Web pages. We tell you all about finding and using images as well as including images that you create yourself. We also make some recommendations about how you should (and should not) use images in your Web pages.

If you're feeling creative and want to make your own images, you need to be comfortable using an image editing or paint program. If you consider yourself artistically impaired, however, you can always use existing images from the Internet or other places.

See also Part II before beginning this part if you need a quick recap of basic tags. Most of the examples in this part include only the tags and attributes discussed in this part and do not include structure or body tags.

In this part . . .

- ✔ **Including images in your documents**
- ✔ **Helping images load more quickly**
- ✔ **Controlling image alignment**
- ✔ **Using images as links**
- ✔ **Creating imagemaps (those cool clickable images)**

Adding Images

You can easily add images to your HTML documents. (Whenever we talk about adding images, we mean including all sorts of pictures, drawings, or diagrams in your HTML documents.)

You include all these images by using either *GIF* (usually pronounced *jiff*) or *JPG* (pronounced *jay-peg*) file formats. Both GIF and JPG images are compressed to take up less disk space and require less downloading time than do many other image formats. GIF images are best for line drawings or images with only a few colors. JPG images are preferable for photographic images or images with fancy shading.

For most purposes, using the GIF file format is best because all graphical browsers can interpret and display GIF files. If, however, you're including, say, a photograph or another image that takes up a lot of disk space, you should strongly consider using the JPG file format. Although not quite all browsers can interpret this format (*most* can, however), JPG files are considerably smaller in terms of disk space and, therefore, don't take f-o-r-e-v-e-r to download to your readers' browsers.

An up-and-coming new graphic format, called *PNG* (and pronounced *ping*), is probably going to gain in popularity in the near future. This format, which is usable only on the newest browsers, combines the advantages of JPG and GIF images and could be worth considering for your future image needs.

Adding images isn't too complicated — just include a correctly formed <IMG> tag and the SRC="...." attribute, which points to a valid URL (either absolute or relative) for your image.

See also Part III for more information about partial or absolute URLs.

The following table shows some of the common image-related tags and attributes:

HTML Tag or Attribute	*Effect*	*Use in Pairs?*
<IMG SRC="....">	Inserts an image.	No
ALT="...."	Specifies text to display if image isn't displayed.	No
BORDER=n	Controls thickness of border around an image in pixels.	No

The following example shows you how to add an image to your document.

Note: Before beginning, make sure that you have your browser and text editor open and ready to create a new document. Or you can apply this information to an existing document. You should also have an image available to use in the document.

To include an image in your document, follow these steps:

1. Start your HTML page.

We start with the following sample of HTML code:

```
<!DOCTYPE HTML PUBLIC "-//W3C//DTD HTML 3.2
    Final//EN">
<HTML>
<HEAD><TITLE>Cat Gallery</TITLE></HEAD>
<BODY>
<H1>Cats in Our Lives (for Better or Worse)
    </H1>
<P>We've got several cats that figure
    prominently in our lives, including:</P>
<UL>
<LI>Winchester
<LI>Lucy
<LI>Booker
</UL>
</BODY>
</HTML>
```

2. Add the <IMG> tag wherever you want your image to appear, as in the following example:

```
<P>We've got several cats that figure
    prominently in our lives, including:</P>
<IMG>
```

3. Add the SRC= attribute to provide the address of the image, as the following example shows.

(The image we're using is called winchest.gif, and it's located in the same folder as our HTML document.)

```
<IMG SRC="winchest.gif">
```

4. Add the ALT= attribute to describe the image, just in case the viewer can't view (or chooses not to view) the image, as follows:

```
<IMG SRC="winchest.gif" ALT="Winchester the
    Cat">
```

The resulting Web page looks like the following figure.

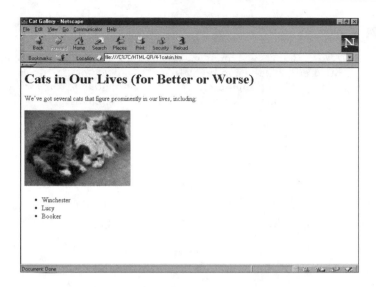

Technically, you don't need to provide the ALT text (which stands for *alternative text*) with the image; however, doing so is a good idea. Sometimes people use browsers that can't display images. Many people also commonly stop their browsers from showing images so that they don't need to wait for the images to copy to their computer over a slow modem connection. By using ALT, you tell them what they're missing instead of making them guess. Also, many browsers use the ALT text for those cute little popup tips that appear when you hover your mouse over the image.

The following figure shows an example of how the ALT text may look to readers viewing the same page without the images.

Creating images for HTML documents

Creating images for your HTML documents isn't really any more difficult than creating other images. You create the image and save it in a specific file format.

As you're creating images for HTML documents, keep in mind that some colors work better than others. Check the following section, "Choosing colors carefully," for information about choosing colors for use in HTML documents.

The following example shows you how to create appropriate images to use in HTML documents.

Note: You need to be familiar with how to use a drawing or image-editing program to create images. You could use anything from Adobe Photoshop to Microsoft PowerPoint to the drawing tools in your word-processing program to develop images. Whichever program(s) you choose, you need to make sure that at least one of them can save images in GIF or JPG format.

To create images appropriate for use in HTML documents, follow these steps:

1. Create an image that you want to use in your HTML document.

2. In the program you use to create the image, click File⇨Save As (or on File⇨Export or something similar) to save the image as a GIF or JPG image.

3. Type a name and a location in your Save As dialog box.

   Make sure that the image type you select is either GIF or JPG and that the location is the same as your HTML documents (for ease of linking).

If your favorite drawing program doesn't save in either GIF or JPG format, you can try either of the following approaches:

✦ Save the image as a TIF image and import the file into a program that can save it in GIF or JPG format. Paint Shop Pro or LView for Windows, Graphic Converter for Macintosh, and xv for UNIX are some possible candidates.

✦ Copy the image from the creation program (by selecting the image and choosing Edit⇨Copy from the menu bar) and then paste the image into the other program, the one that can save in the correct format (by choosing Edit⇨Paste from that program's menu bar).

This second procedure works well if you have a photo-editing program such as Photoshop or Paint Shop Pro (which can save in the right format) but you're more comfortable being creative in a different program, such as PowerPoint (which does not save individual images in the correct format).

Choosing colors carefully

Good color choices are ones that look good in practically any browser and operating system and display resolution configuration — that is, they show up clearly, not splotchy or mottled. Unfortunately, color involves more than meets the eye.

The following information about choosing colors applies not only to image colors, but also applies to background colors (which we cover in Part V).

As you're choosing colors, keep in mind that not all colors are created equally. Some colors don't show up at all in readers' browsers; if you choose a color from the 16.7 million-color palette, for example, and your readers' browsers are set to only 256 colors, the color you choose may not show up crisp and clear if it isn't one of the 256. For that matter, even if you choose a color from the 256-color palette, the color could show up splotchy (a condition technically called *dithered*) on many readers' screens.

To figure out which colors to use, you should first know how colors are determined. Colors are specified by an *RGB* (Red-Green-Blue) number. By using three numbers (either three decimal numbers or three two-digit hex numbers), you can specify the amounts of red, green, and blue to include to create any one of about 16.7 million colors. By mixing the levels of RGB, you can create any color you want.

So which colors are best to use in HTML documents? Colors that are standard across all platforms and that look good even at lower color resolutions. How do you know which ones? Fortunately, we have a list and color samples on the Cheat Sheet in the front of the book. Choose colors with the values from the tables in the following sections for the best results. By using these values to choose colors (pick one number from each column to create the RGB number), you stand the best chance of having those colors show up clearly in just about any browser.

If your image editing software uses hexadecimal numbers . . .

The following table provides values you can use if your image editing software uses hexadecimal numbers. You also use the hexadecimal numbers for specifying colors within your HTML documents (say, for the background). *See also* Part V for details.

The *hexadecimal numbering system (hex)* provides you with the same values as the decimal system does, but hex uses 16 digits instead of 10. The digits for hex are 0–9 and the letters A–F in place of the numbers 10–15. By using two hex digits (##), you can specify a number between 0 (00) and 255 (FF).

Use the following table like you would a Chinese menu (one from column Red, one from column Green, and one from column Blue) to choose two-digit color numbers.

Hexadecimal Color Selections

Red	Green	Blue
00	00	00
33	33	33
66	66	66
99	99	99
CC	CC	CC
FF	FF	FF

You may, for example, choose hexadecimal #336699 or #CC00CC or #FFFFFF to make fairly sure that the color looks pure on most displays. The hex number FF0000 is Red, 00FF00 is Green, and 0000FF is Blue. White is equal amounts of each color (because you're working with light), so you can create it by choosing FFFFFF. Black, on the other hand, uses no color at all and is 000000.

If your image editing software uses decimal numbers . . .

The following table provides values you can use if your image editing software uses decimal RGB numbers to set colors. Again, think Chinese menu — take a number from column Red, another number from column Green, and the final number from column Blue.

Decimal Color Selections

Red	Green	Blue
0	0	0
51	51	51
102	102	102
153	153	153
204	204	204
255	255	255

You may, for example, choose a RGB color such as decimal 0, 51, 102 — or perhaps 204, 153, 255 — to make fairly sure that the color looks good on displays that show only 256 colors. The RGB color 0, 0, 0 is black, for example, while 255, 0, 0 is red, and 255, 255, 255 is white.

Borrowing images

Borrowing images from other Web pages helps provide you with ideas and gives you materials that you can use to *practice* including images in your documents.

Of course, we don't recommend using other people's images in your public Web pages (both because of copyright laws and because doing so is just plain wrong). Remember that whoever created the image you're borrowing holds the copyright to it. Don't just take the image and use it in your own documents. Of course, if the image is clearly labeled as one that you're free to use in your own pages and you know that the individual or group giving permission has the right to give that permission, you're in the clear.

A number of very good sites on the Internet offer clip art or Web art that's free for noncommercial use. Check out Yahoo! (at `http://www.yahoo.com`) and search for **clip art**. You find all you could ever use.

The following procedure shows you how to borrow images from other documents on the Web.

Note: Before beginning, make sure that you have your browser open.

To borrow images off the Web, follow these steps:

1. Find an HTML document that you like on the Web.

   (You can perform this step as often as you want, so don't be too picky.)

2. Using the right mouse button, click the image that you want to copy.

   A pop-up menu appears providing several options. (*Note:* If you're a Macintosh user, you just click and hold the mouse button for a couple of seconds.)

3. Choose the Save This Image As option from the pop-up menu.

   (Although the option in your program may not be worded exactly as shown here, it should be similar.)

4. Type a name and a location in your Save As dialog box and click <u>S</u>ave.

   Again, you make your life easier if you choose the same location (folder) as that in which you keep your HTML documents.

Creating transparent images

A *transparent image* is one in which the background color doesn't show up — it's replaced by the background color that's visible in the browser. Consider making your images transparent if the background is likely to be a distraction or if the important part of your image is not rectangular. Take a look at the following figure, which shows an image with a regular background (at top) and the same image with a transparent background (bottom).

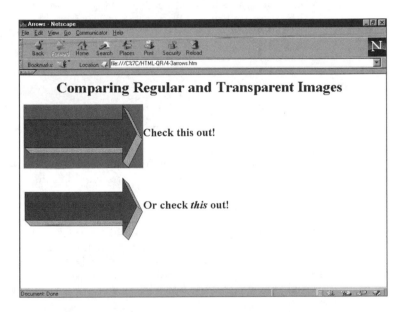

If you want to use transparent backgrounds, you must save them as GIF images, Version *89a*. You should have selections in your Save As dialog box that let you select both GIF and the specific version number — Version 87a or 89a — as you're saving your GIF image. JPG images *cannot* be transparent.

Many graphics or photo-editing software packages allow you to easily make a background color transparent. If you don't have photo-editing software and don't want to invest in it, you can check out freeware and shareware programs available on the Internet. Many of these programs offer menu options for choosing the background color (that is, the color that disappears in the browser).

To create transparent images, use a procedure similar to the following one. In these steps, we don't address the specifics for a particular software package; instead, we give you the general process for using any package.

Note: Before beginning, be sure that you have your image editing software open and ready to use.

Follow these steps:

1. Open a GIF image in your graphics software program.

   Note: The image must have a uniform background color.

2. Locate your options for selecting a background color.

   Many programs have a Background Color option under one of the menus, but this option varies greatly from program to program. (In Paint Shop Pro, for example, select the dropper tool and then right-click the background color.)

3. Select the existing background color (the one you want to be transparent).

4. Go to the Save As dialog box and type in a name and a location.

   (Make sure that you save the image as a GIF 89a image!)

5. Look for Save As options (probably accessible by clicking an Options button) and select an option that specifies "Make Background Color Transparent" or something similar.

At this point, you don't see a change in the image background — you must open the image in your browser to see the results of your hard work. In any case, you should go ahead and view the image in your browser just to make sure that the image looks how you want it to look. In your browser, choose File⇨Open or File⇨Open Page, select Show All Files at the bottom of the dialog box that appears, find the image file you want to view, and then click Open.

Adding Images as Anchors

You can use images as your anchors for making links. Using images as anchors isn't any more complicated than first creating a link and, second, adding an image.

The following example shows you how to use an image as an anchor to link to another document.

Note: Before beginning, make sure that you have your browser and text editor open and ready to create a new document. Or you can apply this information to an existing document. You should have an image available to use in your document and another document available to which to link.

To use an image as the anchor to link to another document, follow these steps:

1. Start your HTML document.

Your document may look similar to the following example:

```
<!DOCTYPE HTML PUBLIC "-//W3C//DTD HTML 3.2
   Final//EN">
<HTML>
<HEAD><TITLE>Cat Gallery</TITLE></HEAD>
<BODY>
<H1>Cats in Our Lives (for Better or Worse)
   </H1>
<P>We've got several cats that figure
   prominently in our lives, including:</P>
<UL>
<LI>Winchester
<LI>Lucy
<LI>Booker
</UL>
</BODY>
</HTML>
```

2. Add a link, as shown in the following example.

```
<P>
<UL>
<LI>Winchester <A HREF="winchbio.html">
   (Biography)</A>
<LI>Lucy
<LI>Booker
</UL>
```

See also Part III if you need a review on adding links.

3. Add the <IMG> tag where you want the image to appear, as follows:

```
<P>
<UL>
<LI>Winchester <A HREF="winchbio.html">
   <IMG>(Biography)</A>
<LI>Lucy
<LI>Booker
</UL>
```

4. Add the SRC attribute to the <IMG> tag, as follows.

(This attribute tells what graphic you're including in your HTML document.)

```
<P>
<UL>
<LI>Winchester <A HREF="winchbio.html">
   <IMG SRC="winchest.jpg">(Biography)</A>
<LI>Lucy
<LI>Booker
</UL>
```

5. Add the ALT attribute to the <IMG> tag, as shown in the following example.

(This attribute tells what text to display if the image isn't displayed.)

```
<P>
<UL>
<LI>Winchester <A HREF="winchbio.html">
    <IMG SRC="winchest.jpg" ALT="Link to
    Winchester's Biography">(Biography)</A>
<LI>Lucy
<LI>Booker
</UL>
```

The Web page looks something like the following figure.

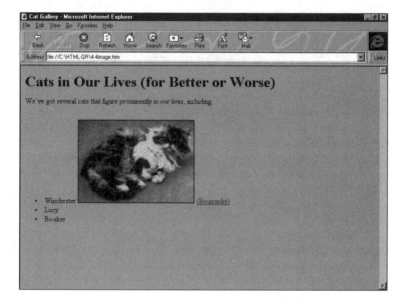

Notice that the image in this example has a border around it. The border is the same color as other links in the document, which indicates to your readers that the image links to other information or files.

If you don't want the border around the image, you can add the BORDER=0 attribute to the <IMG> tag. Without any visual cues, however, your readers probably won't know that the image is a link. Just make sure that your intent is clearly communicated to your readers.

You don't need to leave the text in the anchor (Biography, in this example) if you don't want to. Telling your readers what they're linking to, however, is a good idea. You can give them this information by providing cues, such as text, in the link itself or in the surrounding text.

Addressing Image Download Speed

Images take quite a while to download (particularly over a slow Internet connection), and your readers are likely to give up on your Web site and move on if the images take too long to appear on-screen. (By the way, this situation is why the Web is often called the "World Wide Wait.") If you're on a fast Internet connection or if you're testing your HTML documents directly from your hard drive (as most of us do), you probably don't notice how long some images take to load, but a 28.8 Kbps modem (which is pretty standard) takes a long time to transfer images — sometimes up to several minutes.

Basically, you can shorten the "World Wide Wait" in any of the following three ways:

+ You can reduce the image file size.

+ You can use a thumbnail image, which is just a smaller image that links to the full-size image.

+ You can indicate image dimensions in the HTML document.

Reducing file size

One of the best ways you can help speed image download time is to reduce the image file size. The following techniques can help reduce image file size and make an incredible difference in how fast they load:

+ **Reduce color depth.** Check your image-editing software for options such as Reduce Color Depth. For fairly simple graphics, reducing the color depth to 16 colors, instead of 256 colors or millions of colors, can make the image much smaller with little or no visible difference in the image.

+ **Use the JPG format for photographs.** Remember that the JPG file format compresses photographs and complex images more than the GIF format does. Additionally, programs that allow you to save by using JPG format also offer a place to set compression options. Experiment with the compression and increase compression until you start to see a loss of quality; then back off a little.

Because JPG compression is *lossy* — meaning that some of the data comprising the photograph is actually discarded during compression — try to avoid recompressing already compressed images. If you compress, recompress, and then recompress again, you may end up with *artifacts,* which are funny markings within the image. Better to compress only one time with the correct compression ratio — that is, try a compression of, say, 10. If it looks fine, undo the compression or revert to the original image and then try 20.

✦ **Use the** LOWSRC=". . ." **attribute in the image tag in addition to the regular** SRC=". . ." **attribute.** (The code would look something like <IMG LOWSRC="verycompressed. jpg" SRC="regular.gif">.) The LOWSRC= attribute points to a very highly compressed JPG file (that is, a very small one) that has the same dimensions as the image pointed to by SRC=. The very small image loads first and gives readers something to look at while the larger (main) image loads. This attribute works only in Netscape Navigator but does not cause any problems on other browsers, so it may be worth trying.

Using thumbnails

Thumbnail images are very small copies of bigger images linked to those bigger images. Readers seeing a page full of thumbnail images get the idea of what the pictures look like, but don't need to wait all day for the bigger images to download.

We'd particularly recommend using thumbnails if you have many images or very large images in a page or if the images really stand alone and aren't necessary to support the surrounding text. Using thumbnails in this way isn't any more complicated than is making a link and adding an image.

The following example shows you how to use a thumbnail to link to a larger image.

Note: Before beginning, make sure that you have your browser and text editor open and ready to create a new document. Or you can apply this information to an existing document. You should have an image available to link into your document and another document available to which to link. You also need to have ready a thumbnail-sized image (about 100 x 100 pixels or less), which you link to your full-sized image.

To use a thumbnail image as the hot spot for linking to a larger image, follow these steps:

1. Start your HTML document.

The document should look something like the following example:

```
<!DOCTYPE HTML PUBLIC "-//W3C//DTD HTML 3.2
  Final//EN">
<HTML>
<HEAD><TITLE>Cat Gallery</TITLE></HEAD>
<BODY>
<H1>Cats in Our Lives (for Better or Worse)
  </H1>
<P>We've got several cats that figure
  prominently in our lives, including:</P>
<UL>
<LI>Winchester
<LI>Lucy
<LI>Booker
</UL>
</BODY>
</HTML>
```

2. Add an `<IMG>` tag, complete with `SRC=` and `ALT=` attributes, as follows.

(This attribute should point to the thumbnail — the smaller image.)

```
<UL>
<LI>Winchester <IMG SRC="winthumb.jpg"
  ALT="Winchester Thumbnail">
<LI>Lucy
<LI>Booker
</UL>
```

3. Add anchor tags around the image, as follows:

```
<UL>
<LI>Winchester <A><IMG SRC="winthumb.jpg"
  ALT="Winchester Thumbnail"></A>
<LI>Lucy
<LI>Booker
</UL>
```

4. Add the `HREF` attribute, as the following example shows.

This attribute should point to the larger image.

```
<UL>
<LI>Winchester <A HREF="winbig.gif">
  <IMG SRC="winthumb.jpg" ALT="Winchester
  Thumbnail"></A>
<LI>Lucy
<LI>Booker
</UL>
```

Your result looks somewhat like the following figure.

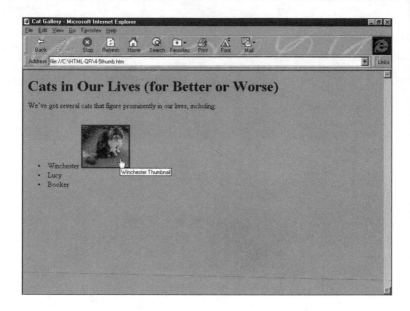

Notice that the image in this example has a border around it. The border is the same color as the color of other links in the document. This border tells your readers that the image links to something. (*Note:* We increased the border size by using the instructions from the following section so that the border would be clear in this illustration.)

In this example, we chose to use a very small, very highly compressed (and, therefore, low-quality) JPG format image as the thumbnail so that the page loads quickly. The thumbnail links to a much larger and higher-quality image. We assume that if people like Winchester's picture enough to try to view the larger one, they don't mind waiting for a big image to load.

You can choose not to have the colored border appear around the thumbnail (or around all other images used as an anchor). Just add the BORDER attribute to the <IMG> tag with a value of 0 — BORDER=0, as shown in the following example.

Note: This example builds on the previous one.

```
<UL>
<LI>Winchester <A HREF="winbig.gif">
   <IMG SRC="winthumb.gif" ALT="Winchester
   Thumbnail" BORDER=0></A>
<LI>Lucy
<LI>Booker
</UL>
```

The following figure shows the same thumbnail without the border.

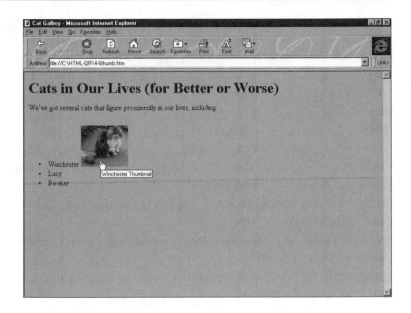

 If you remove the border, your readers don't necessarily know that the image is a link because no visual cues indicate that they are to click the image. Removing a border is a neat trick, but it's not always a good idea.

Specifying image size

You can improve how fast images *seem* to load by specifying the dimensions of the image in the HTML code. In doing so, browsers leave space for the image, finish loading the text (at which point your readers can start reading), and then continue loading the images. The images don't actually load faster, but specifying image size can help readers think they're loading faster, which is almost as good.

You specify the dimensions of the image (generally displayed in the title bar or status bar of image-editing programs) by including height and width attributes in the <IMG> tag. The numbers you specify for height and width specify the size in *pixels,* which are those itty-bitty dots on-screen that make up the image. (If you look really close at your screen, you can actually see the little pixels — aren't they tiny?!)

The following table shows the attributes used to specify image height and width.

HTML Attributes	Effect	Use in Pairs?
HEIGHT=n	Specifies the height of the image in pixels.	No
WIDTH=n	Specifies the width of the image in pixels.	No

The following example shows you how to include image dimensions in an <IMG> tag.

Note: Before beginning, make sure that you have your browser and text editor open with an HTML document loaded. You should have an image in the document as well.

To include the dimensions of the image in an <IMG> tag, follow these steps:

1. Open the image in your image-editing software and find the dimensions.

These dimensions probably appear in the title bar at the top of the window or in the status bar at the bottom of the window. They're generally given as horizontal and then vertical.

2. Add the WIDTH and HEIGHT attributes, as follows:

```
<!DOCTYPE HTML PUBLIC "-//W3C//DTD HTML 3.2
   Final//EN">
<HTML>
<HEAD><TITLE>Lucy Looks</TITLE></HEAD>
<BODY>
<H1>Look, Lucy, Look!</H1>
<P><IMG SRC="lucy2a.gif" ALT="Lucy Looking
   Right" WIDTH=200 HEIGHT=157>
Lucy liked checking out interesting stuff when
   she was a kitten.</P>
</BODY>
</HTML>
```

You haven't really changed anything's appearance; these attributes just help the page appear to load more quickly by telling the browser what size image to expect.

Controlling Image Alignment

Just as you can control how big or small an image is, you can also control how the images align with other elements on the page. By default, browsers align images on the left side of the page. If you want, you can realign them so that the images appear aligned at the right, or aligned vertically, as you want. (If you're going to use alignment attributes, make sure that your readers don't use completely antiquated browsers.)

The following table shows the attributes used to control image alignment.

HTML Attribute	Effect	Use in Pairs?
ALIGN="bottom"	Aligns the bottom of the image with the baseline of the current line.	No
ALIGN="left"	Allows an image to float down and over to the left margin (into the next available space); subsequent text wraps to the right of that image.	No
ALIGN="middle"	Aligns the baseline of the current line with the middle of the image.	No
ALIGN="right"	Aligns the image with the right margin and wraps the text around the left.	No
ALIGN="top"	Aligns the text with the top of the tallest item in the line.	No
HSPACE=n	Controls the horizontal space (white space) around the image in pixels.	No
VSPACE=n	Controls the vertical space (white space) around the image in pixels.	No

All you need to do is include these attributes in the <IMG> tag in your HTML document. The order of the attributes within the <IMG> tag isn't important. You can put them in the order that you find most convenient. The following sections show you how to use the various alignment options.

Changing alignment

The following example shows you how to change image alignment.

Note: Before beginning, make sure that you have your browser and text editor open and ready to create a new document. Or you can apply this information to an existing document. You should have an image available to include in this document.

To change the alignment of your image in relation to the surrounding text, follow these steps:

1. Start your HTML document.

We started with a basic HTML document similar to the following example:

```
<!DOCTYPE HTML PUBLIC "-//W3C//DTD HTML 3.2
    Final//EN">
<HTML>
<HEAD><TITLE>Lucy Looks</TITLE></HEAD>
<BODY>
<H1>Look, Lucy, Look!</H1>
<P>Lucy liked checking out interesting stuff
    when she was a kitten. Actually, she was
    pretty much a pain. Not only did she look at
    everything, she got into everything. We were
    just discussing the number of times she
    climbed up the screen door, only to get stuck
    at the very top. Of course, now she's a fatso
    and would tear the door down if she even
    tried to climb up it. What's more, now that
    she's grown, she's also afraid of her own
    shadow. After she leaked outside the other
    day, she spent the next 30 minutes yowling
    and slinking around the house as if the
    beetles were after her. </P>
</BODY>
</HTML>
```

Note: The term "leaked" in these examples describes the way cats move into or out of the house — in whichever direction they're not supposed to go. It's a bit technical, but we thought that using the correct term was preferable to "sneaked" outside. (For all you who wondered whose flower bed was violated, shame on you!)

2. Add the <IMG> tag along with the SRC and ALT attributes, as follows:

```
<H1>Look, Lucy, Look!</H1>
<P><IMG SRC="lucy.jpg" ALT="Lucy Looking
    Right">
Lucy liked checking out interesting stuff when
    she was a kitten. Actually, she was pretty much
    a pain. Not only did she look at everything,
    she got into everything. We were just
    discussing the number of times she climbed up
    the screen door, only to get stuck at the very
    top. Of course, now she's a fatso and would
    tear the door down if she even tried to climb
    up it. What's more, now that she's grown, she's
    also afraid of her own shadow. After she leaked
    outside the other day, she spent the next 30
    minutes yowling and slinking around the house
    as if the beetles were after her. </P>
```

The following figure shows the result of this initial alignment of image and text.

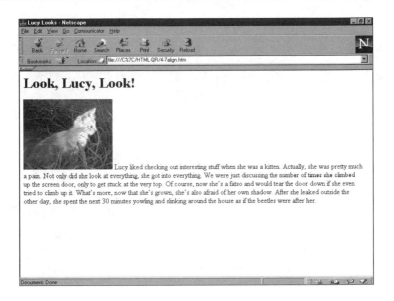

3. Add the `ALIGN` attribute, as shown in the following example.

Start by using `ALIGN="LEFT"`. (This attribute allows your text to wrap around to the right of the image.) The next figure shows the result of this change in alignment between text and image.

```
<P><IMG SRC="lucy.jpg" ALT="Lucy Looking Right"
ALIGN="LEFT">
```

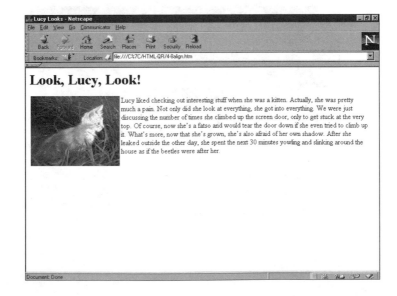

Using multiple alignment options

If you insert several of the tags at once, you can see the differences in the effects. This example includes three images with ALIGN="bottom", ALIGN="middle", and ALIGN="top", respectively and adds the boldface text.

Note: This example builds on the same basic document used in the previous example.

```
<H1>
<IMG SRC="lucysm.jpg" ALT="Lucy Looking Right"
   ALIGN="bottom">Look,
<IMG SRC="lucysm.jpg" ALT="Lucy Looking Right"
   ALIGN="middle">Lucy,
<IMG SRC="lucysm.jpg" ALT="Lucy Looking Right"
   ALIGN="top">Look!</H1>
<P>Lucy liked checking out interesting stuff when
   she was a kitten. Actually, she was pretty much
   a pain. Not only did she look at everything,
   she got into everything. We were just
   discussing the number of times she climbed up
   the screen door, only to get stuck at the very
   top. Of course, now she's a fatso and would
   tear the door down if she even tried to climb
   up it. What's more, now that she's grown, she's
   also afraid of her own shadow. After she leaked
   outside the other day, she spent the next 30
   minutes yowling and slinking around the house
   as if the beetles were after her. </P>
```

The following figure shows the results of each type of alignment.

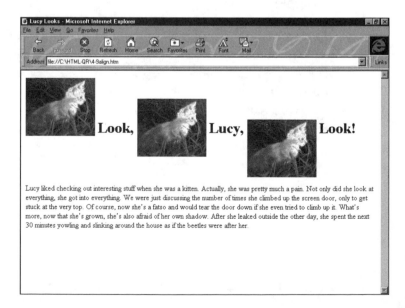

Experiment with the alignment tags until you find the most effective ones for your particular case.

Common browsers generally display most of these tags correctly. Here, as with most other HTML features, we recommend checking the tags by using two or three browsers.

Using alignment to create interesting effects

You can also insert several images by using complementary ALIGN attributes to produce interesting layout effects. (Unfortunately, you have no way to flip images in HTML — we used an image-editing program to make a mirror image of the first one.) The following example shows how to add a second image with right alignment to complement the existing image.

Note: This example builds on the same basic document that the previous example used.

```
<H1>Look, Lucy, Look!</H1>
<IMG SRC="lucy.jpg" ALT="Lucy Looking Right"
   ALIGN="left">
<IMG SRC="lucy1.jpg" ALT="Lucy Looking Left"
   ALIGN="right">
Lucy liked checking out interesting stuff when she
   was a kitten. Actually, she was pretty much a
   pain. Not only did she look at everything, she
   got into everything. We were just discussing
   the number of times she climbed up the screen
   door, only to get stuck at the very top. Of
   course, now she's a fatso and would tear the
   door down if she even tried to climb up it.
   What's more, now that she's grown, she's also
   afraid of her own shadow. After she leaked
   outside the other day, she spent the next 30
   minutes yowling and slinking around the house
   as if the beetles were after her. </P>
```

The following figure shows the results of these alignment options.

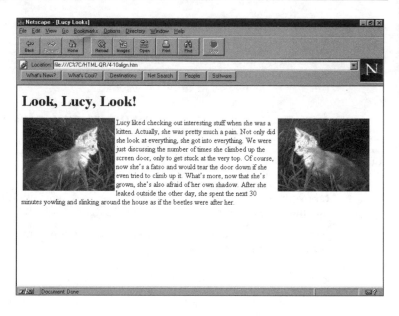

Using horizontal and vertical spacing

You can include these alignment effects by adding vertical and horizontal space around the images.

Just add the HSPACE=n or VSPACE=n attributes (or both). The n is the number of pixels wide that the space should be on each side of the image — thus the total width added is two times n.

Note: This example builds on the previous one by adding extra horizontal space around the existing images.

```
<H1>Look, Lucy, Look!</H1>
<P>
<IMG SRC="lucy.jpg" ALT="Lucy Looking Right"
    ALIGN="left" HSPACE=40>
<IMG SRC="lucy1.jpg" ALT="Lucy Looking Left"
    ALIGN="right" HSPACE=40>
Lucy liked checking out interesting stuff when she
    was a kitten. Actually, she was pretty much a
    pain. Not only did she look at everything, she
    got into everything. We were just discussing
    the number of times she climbed up the screen
    door, only to get stuck at the very top. Of
    course, now she's a fatso and would tear the
    door down if she even tried to climb up it.
    What's more, now that she's grown, she's also
    afraid of her own shadow. After she leaked
    outside the other day, she spent the next 30
    minutes yowling and slinking around the house
    as if the beetles were after her. </P>
```

The following figure shows the results of the extra space around the images.

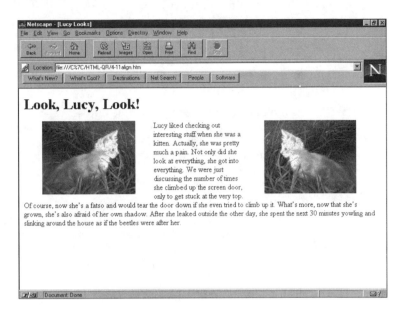

Making Clickable Images

You can use *clickable images* (also called *imagemaps*) to let readers click images or parts of images to link to other pages or images. The imagemap provides a menu of selections for your reader, just as a set of regular links can be a menu for your reader.

Imagemaps are good for making spiffy-looking menus — that is, so that readers can click various parts of an image to link to different information. They're also good for making geographic-related links (by letting people click the state or country of their choice) or for all kinds of orientation or training applications (by allowing people to click get more information about whatever is pictured).

The map controls are run either by browser software (in a *client-side imagemap* — that is, an imagemap controlled by the browser) or by server software (an older, less-efficient, *server-side imagemap* — that is, an imagemap controlled by the Web server).

Keep in mind that older browsers (software, not people) can't use client-side imagemaps, and text-only browsers can't use image-maps at all. Users of older browsers can see the image, but they can't link to other information by clicking the image. Therefore, be sure to include text-based links to supplement your imagemap.

Including imagemaps in your HTML document is fairly easy. The processes for including client-side and server-side imagemaps are very similar. Just follow these steps:

1. Add an image to your HTML document.

2. Define clickable areas (a process called mapping).

3. Define the map — that is, specify which imagemap areas link to what information.

The main difference between client-side and server-side imagemaps is that server-side imagemaps require some help from your system administrator. Because we can't guess how your system administrator has set up server-side imagemaps, we cover only client-side imagemaps in this book. Check with your system administrator for the server-side specifics.

If you decide to provide either kind of imagemap in your HTML document, particularly client-side imagemaps, you should also include an alternative means of navigating your documents (such as text links or buttons). Remember that not all your readers can or choose to use the imagemaps, so they need text links or buttons to navigate.

The following table shows the tags used to add an imagemap to an HTML document.

HTML Tag or Attribute	Effect	Use in Pairs?
`<IMG SRC=". . .">`	Inserts an image.	No
ISMAP	Specifies that the image is a server-side clickable imagemap.	No
USEMAP="#mapname"	Identifies the picture as a client-side imagemap and specifies a MAP to use for acting on the users' clicks.	No

The SRC=". . ." attribute still points to a valid URL (relative or absolute) for your image. The remaining information points to an addition to the HTML document. And all the other valid IMG attributes also apply to your imagemap.

Adding the image

The image you find or create to use in the imagemap should be as clear and as small as you can make it. Stick to a few colors and think simple. Although your readers may be impressed with a graphical masterpiece the first time they see it, they quickly tire of waiting for it to load each time they view your page.

We created the following simple image to illustrate some of the possibilities of imagemaps.

This example shows you how to include the image in your HTML document.

Note: Before beginning, Make sure that you have your browser and text editor open with an HTML document loaded. You should have an image ready to use as well. We start with the following HTML document:

```
<!DOCTYPE HTML PUBLIC "-//W3C//DTD HTML 3.2
   Final//EN">
<HTML>
<HEAD>
<TITLE>Making Imagemaps</TITLE>
</HEAD>
<BODY>
<H1>Making Imagemaps Can Be Fun!</H1>
The image above is an imagemap. <P>
</BODY>
</HTML>
```

To include the image in your HTML document, follow these steps:

1. Include the image in your document, along with the appropriate ALT= information, by adding the following tags and text to the document:

```
<H1>Making Imagemaps Can Be Fun!</H1>
<IMG ALT="This is a clickable map."
   SRC="imagemap.gif">
The image above is an imagemap.<P>
```

2. Include the USEMAP attribute to indicate that the image is to be a client-side imagemap.

   The USEMAP attribute points to a map by name — we use the name demomap for this example, as follows:

```
<H1>Making Imagemaps Can Be Fun!</H1>
<IMG ALT="This is a clickable map."
   SRC="imagemap.gif" USEMAP="#demomap">
The image above is an imagemap.<P>
```

You just added the image into your document and indicated that it's an imagemap. You can't see much of a difference through your browser — the image looks like any other image that's a link in your document. You must define the map first before the hot spots work. Read on.

Mapping clickable areas

In *mapping* clickable areas, you divide the image into parts that eventually link to other information and pages. Mapping is sort of like taking a picture and carving it up into individual pieces (like puzzle pieces) — each piece represents an individual area that you can then link to something else.

Mapping your image isn't too complicated at all. All points or coordinates are measured from the upper-left corner of the image, in *x,y* coordinates. That point on the image is 0,0 — zero pixels across by zero pixels down. The following image shows the cursor pointing at (focused on?) that spot. Notice that you can see the coordinates (0,0) at the lower left of the window.

See also the section "Specifying Image Size," earlier in this part, for more information about pixels.

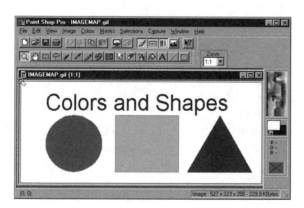

This example identifies the coordinates for each of the three shapes in our sample image. These three shapes show you all you need to know to map all shapes. By identifying the coordinates of certain points in a figure, as described in the following list, you can describe any shapes:

✦ Rectangular shapes require the upper-left and lower-right corners. The computer figures out the rest.

✦ Circles require the center and the radius length. (Yes, you must perform the math to figure out the radius.)

✦ Polygons, such as our triangle, just require each corner. The computer connects the dots to finish the figure.

Any other shape you can represent by using some combination of the rectangle, circle, and polygon. A sleeping cat, for example, can have a long rectangle for the tail, a fatter one for the body, a circle for the head, and a couple of triangles for the ears. Alternatively, you can just go point to point to point on the cat and call it a fancy polygon.

You need to be close on the coordinates, but they don't need to be exact. If you find yourself straining to get the cursor right on the precise point (as we did to get the 0,0 coordinate), you're working too hard. Your readers are just going to point at the image and click — probably not aiming for the very edge. And if you're trying to map lots of shapes or make a clickable map of your city, you should probably check out one of the mapping programs available on the Internet to ease the process. Go to your favorite searching site and look for **imagemap**. We recommend Mapedit for Windows or UNIX and Webmap for Macintosh.

Mapping a rectangle

This section shows how to determine the coordinates for rectangles used in imagemaps.

Note: Before beginning, you should have a sample image open in an image-editing program and have a pencil and paper to note the coordinates.

To determine the coordinates that define a rectangle, follow these steps:

1. Point the cursor at the upper-left corner of the rectangle and write the *x,y* coordinates (208,75), as shown in the following figure.

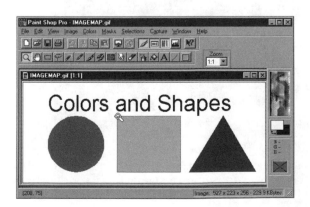

2. Point at the lower-right corner and write the *x,y* coordinates (345,197), as the following figure shows.

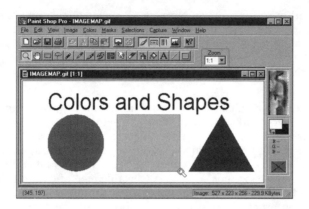

Mapping a circle

This section shows how to determine the coordinates for circles used in imagemaps.

Note: Make sure that you have your sample image open in an image-editing program.

To determine the coordinates of a circle, follow these steps:

1. Point the cursor at the center of the circle, as shown in the following figure, and write the coordinates (118,133, in this example).

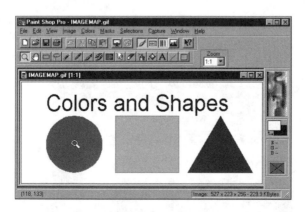

2. Move the cursor horizontally to the edge of the circle, as the following figure shows, and note those coordinates, too (178,133, in this example).

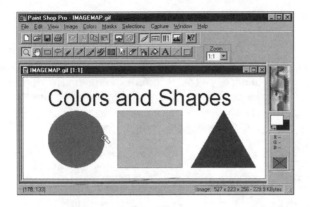

3. Subtract the first *x* coordinate from the second one.

In our example, we subtract 118 from 178 and get 60. That's the radius of the circle.

Mapping a polygon

This section shows how to determine the coordinates for other shapes used in imagemaps.

Note: Make sure that you have your sample image open in an image-editing program.

To determine the coordinates that define the triangle (or any other polygon), follow these steps:

1. Pick a corner and point the cursor at it, as shown in the following figure, and note the *x,y* coordinates.

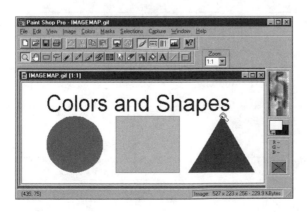

2. Move to the next corner, as the following figure shows, and note those coordinates.

Continue moving around the edge of the shape and noting the coordinates of each corner. Make sure that you mark the corners in order — the computer connects the dots in the same order that you follow to figure out what the shape is.

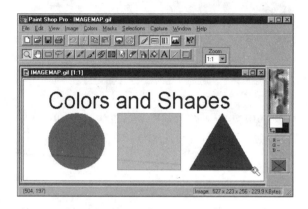

Don't lose the piece of paper with your notes. You need it to define your map.

Defining the map

Defining the map simply tells the computer which areas readers may click and what link to follow after they click. The process looks more complex than it really is. The following table shows the tags and attributes used to define the map.

HTML Tag or Attribute	Effect	Use in Pairs?
`<MAP>. . .</MAP>`	Specifies a collection of hot spots for a client-side imagemap.	Yes
`NAME=". . ."`	Gives the MAP a name so it can be referred to later.	No
`<AREA>`	Specifies the shape of a "hot spot" in a client-side imagemap.	No
`COORDS="x1,y1, x2,y2, . . ."`	Specifies coordinates that define the hot spot's shape.	No
`HREF="URL"`	Specifies the destination of the hot spot.	No
`NOHREF`	Indicates that clicks in this region should cause no action.	No

HTML Tag or Attribute	Effect	Use in Pairs?
SHAPE=". . ."	Specifies type of shape as RECT (for rectangle), CIRC (for circle), or POLY (for polygon).	No

The <MAP>...</MAP> tag tells the browser which areas in your image link to which URLs. This example shows you how to include a map definition in your document along with the imagemap.

Note: Before beginning, make sure that you have your browser and text editor open with an HTML document loaded. You should have an Image in the document as well. We continue here with the previous example:

```
<!DOCTYPE HTML PUBLIC "-//W3C//DTD HTML 3.2
   Final//EN">
<HTML>
<HEAD>
<TITLE>Making Imagemaps</TITLE>
</HEAD>
<BODY>
<H1>Making Imagemaps Can Be Fun!</H1>
<IMG ALT="This is a clickable map."
   SRC="imagemap.gif" USEMAP="#demomap"><P>
The image above is an imagemap. <P>
</BODY>
</HTML>
```

To include a map definition in your document along with the imagemap, follow these steps:

1. Include the <MAP> tags in your document, as shown in the following example:

```
<IMG ALT="This is a clickable map."
   SRC="imagemap.gif" USEMAP="#demomap"><P>
The image above is an imagemap. <P>
<MAP>
</MAP>
</BODY>
</HTML>
```

2. Add the NAME= attribute to the <MAP> tag, as the following example shows.

Note: Our example calls the map *demomap*.

```
<IMG ALT="This is a clickable map."
   SRC="imagemap.gif" USEMAP="#demomap"><P>
The image above is an imagemap. <P>
<MAP NAME="demomap">
</MAP>
</BODY>
</HTML>
```

3. Add an `<AREA>` tag between the `<MAP>` tags, as follows.

You eventually have one `<AREA>` tag for each clickable area in your map, but we build them one at a time.

```
<IMG ALT="This is a clickable map."
   SRC="imagemap.gif" USEMAP="#demomap"><P>
The image above is an imagemap. <P>
<MAP NAME="demomap">
<AREA>
</MAP>
```

4. Add a `SHAPE=` attribute to the `<AREA>` tag, as follows.

We're starting with `SHAPE="RECT"` because the square (rectangle) is the easiest one to do.

```
<IMG ALT="This is a clickable map."
   SRC="imagemap.gif" USEMAP="#demomap"><P>
The image above is an imagemap. <P>
<MAP NAME="demomap">
<AREA SHAPE="RECT">
</MAP>
```

5. Add the `COORDS=` attribute to the `<AREA>` tag, as shown in the following example.

The coordinates for our square are 208,75 for the upper-left corner and 345,197 for the lower-right corner.

```
<IMG ALT="This is a clickable map."
   SRC="imagemap.gif" USEMAP="#demomap"><P>
The image above is an imagemap. <P>
<MAP NAME="demomap">
<AREA SHAPE="RECT" COORDS="208,75,345,197">
</MAP>
```

Note: Do not include spaces between the coordinates.

6. Add the `HREF=` attribute to the `<AREA>` tag, as follows.

You can use any valid URL for your client-side imagemap.

```
<IMG ALT="This is a clickable map."
   SRC="imagemap.gif" USEMAP="#demomap"><P>
The image above is an imagemap. <P>
<MAP NAME="demomap">
<AREA SHAPE="RECT" COORDS="208,75,345,197"
   HREF="/shapes/square.htm">
</MAP>
```

7. Add more `<AREA>` tags as necessary.

Make sure that you include the correct `SHAPE=` and `COORDS=` attributes for each tag. The following example includes the coordinates we noted or calculated in the section "Defining Clickable Areas," earlier in this part.

```
<IMG ALT="This is a clickable map."
  SRC="imagemap.gif" USEMAP="#demomap"><P>
The image above is an imagemap. <P>
<MAP NAME="demomap">
<AREA SHAPE="RECT" COORDS="208,75,345,197"
  HREF="/shapes/square.htm">
<AREA SHAPE="CIRCLE" COORDS="118,33,60"
  HREF="/shapes/round.htm">
<AREA SHAPE="POLYGON"
  COORDS="435,75,504,197,363,196"
  HREF="/shapes/pointy.htm">
</MAP>
```

That's it! Now just load it in your browser and try it out. The result should look something like the following figure.

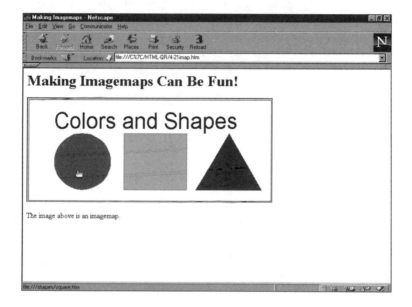

 You can overlap shapes if that helps you to set things up. The first shape that you define in the <MAP> tag is the one that takes precedence. As a matter of fact, a good idea may be to add one final rectangle that covers the entire area of the image with its own link for the people who click in the wrong place.

Part V

Making Effective Web Pages

In this part, we introduce you to some really nifty things that you can do by using HTML — things you can do to help spruce up the ol' humdrum HTML page. And, to help you out, we also provide you with guidelines on how to spruce up your pages effectively.

You need to be pretty familiar with the basic tags before diving into this part. Most of the examples in this part include only the tags and attributes discussed under a particular heading and do not include structure or body tags. We assume that you know where structure and body tags go. If you don't, you may want to refer to Part II of this book.

In this part . . .

- ✔ Using colors and images in backgrounds
- ✔ Changing text colors
- ✔ Moving text around on the page
- ✔ Specifying font size, typeface, and color
- ✔ Breaking lines and pages
- ✔ Making tables
- ✔ Providing author and contact information

Adding a Color Background

You, too, can use color backgrounds in your Web page — it's not reserved for those high-tech supersites. Keep in mind that not all browsers support background colors (but most of the newest ones do), so the possibility exists that your well-crafted background may not show up for some readers.

To include a background color, all you need to do is insert the BGCOLOR= attribute in the opening <BODY> tag.

The following table shows the attribute used to specify background color in an HTML document.

HTML Attribute (for the <BODY> tag)	Effect	Use in Pairs?
BGCOLOR="#rrggbb" or name	Specifies the color number of the background.	No

This example shows you how to add a background color.

Note: Before beginning the example in this section, make sure that you have your browser and text editor open and ready to create a new document. Or you can apply this information to an existing document.

To use a color background, follow these steps:

1. Start your HTML page.

The page should look something like the following example:

```
<!DOCTYPE HTML PUBLIC "-//W3C//DTD HTML 3.2
  Final//EN">
<HTML>
<HEAD><TITLE>Fleabag Kitty</TITLE></HEAD>
<BODY>With a scratcha scratcha here and a
  scratcha scratcha there . . .
</BODY>
</HTML>
```

2. Add the BGCOLOR attribute to the <BODY> tag.

For the following example, we use *#3399CC* (which is sky blue):

```
<HEAD><TITLE>Fleabag Kitty</TITLE></HEAD>
<BODY BGCOLOR="#3399CC">With a scratcha
  scratcha here and a scratcha scratcha
  there . . .
</BODY>
```

The following figure shows the results of this change.

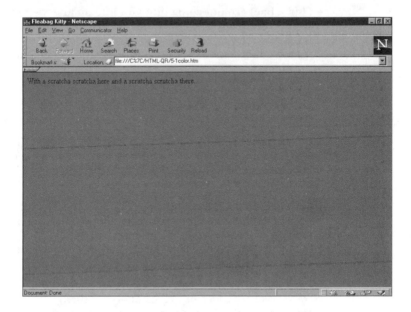

In the place of #RRGGBB, insert a *hexadecimal number* — just a combination of letters and numbers that means something to the computer but means something to you only with the help of a crib sheet (like the Cheat Sheet inside this book's front cover). To get a black background, for example, you use #000000. (If you specify a black background, look at the following section to specify colors for the text.)

See also Part IV, the section called "Choosing Colors Carefully," about choosing hexadecimal RGB numbers appropriate for using in HTML documents.

Alternatively, you can specify some colors by name. The following colors work in most browsers: aqua, black, blue, fuchsia, gray, green, lime, maroon, navy, olive, purple, red, silver, teal, white, and yellow. The code would look something like BGCOLOR="purple".

Remember that all text and graphics appear on top of the background; therefore, make sure that the color you choose is light enough so that the text remains easily readable.

Finding RGB values

So just where do you come up with the RGB values? Try one of the following five ways:

◆ **Use the Cheat Sheet at the front of this book.**

◆ **Find a background color that you like on an existing Web page — and copy it!** Most, if not all, browsers provide a way for you to view the HTML page used to create a Web site. Look for the color number in the ⟨BODY⟩ tag for use in your own documents.

Generally, if you're viewing a page from your browser, you can choose View⇨Page Source or View⇨Source to see the HTML codes used to create the document.

◆ **Check out Part IV, the section "Choosing Colors Carefully."** This section provides you with handy dandy information about choosing RGB values and can help you choose ones that look good in almost any browser.

◆ **Find a list of RGB numbers provided on the Web.** If you browse enough on the Web, you're likely to find general sources of information that provide you with lists of commonly used Web page features, including RGB numbers, complete with samples.

◆ **Look for RGB values in your image editing or paint software.** Many of these packages offer you the option of altering the colors with which you're working and provide you with the RGB value for the colors that you choose. Look in the Help screens for RGB values.

Adding an Image Background

In addition to using simple colors for backgrounds, you can use images as backgrounds. The process is similar to adding a color, except that you're adding an entire image. The BACKGROUND attribute expects a URL (relative or absolute) pointing to an image.

The background value is just a standard URL, so if the image is somewhere other than in the same folder as your document, you need to include the relative or absolute URL, not just the filename. The following table shows the attribute used to apply a background image to an HTML document.

HTML Attributes (for the ⟨BODY⟩ tag)	Effect	Use in Pairs?
BACKGROUND=". . ."	Places an image as a background.	No

This example shows you how to use an image for the background of your HTML document.

Note: Before beginning, make sure that you have your browser and text editor open and ready to start a document. You can also apply this information to an existing document.

To use an image for a background, follow these steps:

1. Start your HTML page.

The page should look something like the following example:

```
<!DOCTYPE HTML PUBLIC "-//W3C//DTD HTML 3.2
   Final//EN">
<HTML>
<HEAD><TITLE>Fleabag Kitty</TITLE></HEAD>
<BODY>With a scratcha scratcha here and a
   scratcha scratcha there . . .</BODY>
</HTML>
```

2. Add the BACKGROUND="..." attribute, including an image filename, to the <BODY> tag, as follows:

```
<BODY BACKGROUND="flea.gif">With a scratcha
   scratcha here and a scratcha scratcha
   there . . .</BODY>
```

The following figure shows the flea.gif image (one flea) tiled throughout the page. Yes, it's really a flea, not a roach (ick!).

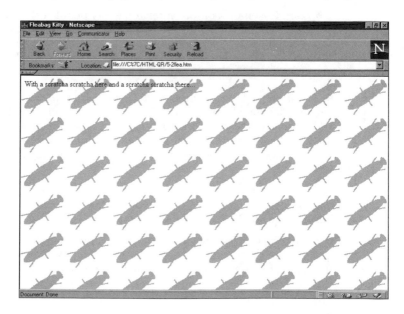

Background images, such as the `flea.gif` image, that do not fill the entire background are *tiled* to cover all the available space — that is, copies of the image are automatically placed together like a tile floor. The background image in the example is really only one flea — the copies are done automatically by the browser.

Finding images to use

Coming up with images to use is about as easy as using simple colors. The only difference is that you use an image file rather than just a color number. Here are some ways to find background images:

✦ **Design your own.** You may want to use a background image that's specific to the Web site you're creating. We strongly suggest doing so if you have any graphics talent at all.

✦ **Find backgrounds that you like on the Web.** Don't just copy these and use them, but you can get good ideas on what looks good and what doesn't.

Keep in mind that copyright laws also apply to the Internet and that the ease of copying images doesn't equate to the appropriateness of doing so.

✦ **Look for image or background CDs or disks in your local software store.** Many CDs are available that have nothing but cool backgrounds.

✦ **Look for images on the Internet.** Many people create images and then put them into the public domain for your use. Again, remember the copyright laws and be aware that having someone else do the copying for you doesn't make the practice right either.

Really good background images are *seamless*. Seamless images look just like one big image if they're used as a background. The key is to make the edges match up evenly. Some image-editing software, such as the newest versions of Paint Shop Pro (check out `http://www.jasc.com` on the Web) can automatically make images seamless.

Make sure that you choose simple backgrounds — ones with no more than two colors and/or with only a few elements. Busy backgrounds make reading difficult for your users.

If you're one of those lucky people with a nice big monitor, high-quality video card, and really spiffy resolution, please take pity on the rest of us. Great background effects for you may be smudgy and unclear to many of us. Check out your effects on a low-end monitor.

If you like backgrounds that provide a vertical band down one side, as shown in the following figure, you can create those backgrounds by making very short (just a few pixels) and very wide (at least 1,280 pixels) images that look like a cross-section of the background effect you want. That image, after you tile it, produces a band down the side of the monitor, as in the following figure.

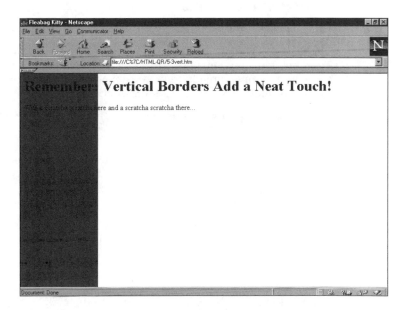

Altering Document Text Colors

In addition to changing the background of Web pages, you can also change the color of the text. This technique is particularly handy if you've used a background on which the default colors of text and links do not show up well. The following table shows the attributes used to color text in an HTML document.

HTML Attribute	Effect	Use in Pairs?
TEXT=#RRGGBB	Changes color of the body text.	No
LINK=#RRGGBB	Changes color of the link.	No
ALINK=#RRGGBB	Changes color of the active link.	No
VLINK=#RRGGBB	Changes color of the visited link.	No

You fill in a color number where `"#RRGGBB"` is indicated. In the following examples, we use `BGCOLOR="#3399CC"`, `TEXT="#FFFFFF"`, `LINK="#FF0000"`, `ALINK="#FFFF00"`, and `VLINK="#8C1717"`. Because colors of text generally don't appear in a large mass, choosing one of the "best" color numbers is far less important for text.

Changing text colors

This example shows you how to change text colors on your Web page.

Note: Before beginning, make sure that you have your browser and text editor open and ready to create a new document. Or you can apply this information to an existing document.

To change text colors on your Web page, follow these steps:

1. Start your HTML page.

The page should look similar to the following example:

```
<!DOCTYPE HTML PUBLIC "-//W3C//DTD HTML 3.2
    Final//EN">
<HTML>
<HEAD><TITLE>Fleabag Kitty</TITLE></HEAD>
<BODY BGCOLOR="#3399CC">With a scratcha
    scratcha here and a scratcha scratcha
    there . . .
</BODY>
</HTML>
```

2. Add the `TEXT="#FFFFFF"` attribute to the `<BODY>` tag to change the color of the body text, as follows:

```
<BODY BGCOLOR="#3399CC" TEXT="#FFFFFF">With a
    scratcha scratcha here and a scratcha
    scratcha there . . .
</BODY>
```

The following figure shows the colored text on a background.

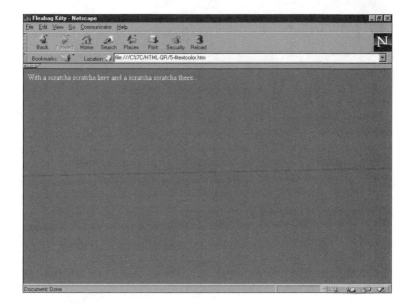

Changing link colors

This example shows you how to change link colors on your Web page.

Note: This example builds on the previous one.

To change link colors on your Web page, use the following steps:

1. Start your HTML page, which should look something like this example:

```
<!DOCTYPE HTML PUBLIC "-//W3C//DTD HTML 3.2
    Final//EN">
<HTML>
<HEAD><TITLE>Fleabag Kitty</TITLE></HEAD>
<BODY BGCOLOR="#3399CC" TEXT="#FFFFFF">With a
    scratcha scratcha here and a scratcha
    scratcha there . . .
</BODY>
</HTML>
```

2. Add LINK="#FF0000" attributes to the <BODY> tag to change the various link colors, as follows:

```
<BODY BGCOLOR="#3399CC" TEXT="#FFFFFF"
    LINK="#FF0000">With a scratcha scratcha here
    and a scratcha scratcha there . . .
</BODY>
```

3. Add `ALINK="#FFFF00"` and `VLINK="#8C1717"` attributes to the `<BODY>` tag to finish changing the link colors, as shown here:

```
<BODY BGCOLOR="#3399CC" TEXT="#FFFFFF"
  LINK="#FF0000" ALINK="#FFFF00"
  VLINK="#8C1717">With a scratcha scratcha here
  and a scratcha scratcha there . . .
</BODY>
```

After you add links to your document and browse through some of them, you see the differences in link color, visited link color, and active link color. Enjoy!

Altering Text Alignment

If you're feeling marginally creative, you may want to move text items around so that they're not all aligned on the left. You can align headings, paragraphs, other text, and images by using the attributes in the following table.

See also Part IV, specifically the section "Controlling Image Alignment," for specifics on image alignment options.

Keep in mind that, although most browsers support these attributes, not all do, so your text may not be aligned correctly in some browsers. Always try out designs in more than one browser to make sure that your design works the way you think it should. The following table presents the attributes used to control text alignment.

HTML Attribute	*Effect*	*Use in Pairs?*
`ALIGN="CENTER"`	Centers text within the left and right margins.	No
`ALIGN="RIGHT"`	Aligns text on the right margin.	No

You don't need to add an attribute if you want the element aligned left. Browsers align text to the left unless you tell them to do otherwise.

If you want to use center and right alignment for headings, paragraphs, and images, follow this example.

Note: Before beginning, make sure that you have your browser and text editor open and ready to create a new document. Or you can apply this information to an existing document.

Follow these steps:

1. Start your HTML page, which should look similar to the following example:

```
<!DOCTYPE HTML PUBLIC "-//W3C//DTD HTML 3.2
    Final//EN">
<HTML>
<HEAD><TITLE>Birthday</TITLE></HEAD>
<BODY>

</BODY>
</HTML>
```

2. Type a heading, as follows:

```
<BODY>
<H1>Happy Birthday, Winchester</H1>
</BODY>
```

3. Add the ALIGN="right" attribute to the heading, as in the following example:

```
<H1 ALIGN="right">Happy Birthday, Winchester
    </H1>
```

4. Insert a graphic on the left side of the heading, as follows:

```
<H1 ALIGN="right"><IMG SRC="winch.jpg">Happy
    Birthday, Winchester</H1>
```

5. Type the following paragraph information:

```
<P>On March 3, Deb and Eric snuck up on their
    cat, Winchester, and surprised him with a
    water balloon for his birthday. It was lucky
    #13 for Winchester.</P>
</BODY>
```

6. Add the ALIGN="center" attribute to the paragraph, as shown here:

```
<P ALIGN="center">On March 3, Deb and Eric
    snuck up on their cat, Winchester, and
    surprised him with a water balloon for his
    birthday. It was lucky #13 for Winchester.
    </P>
```

The following figure shows the result.

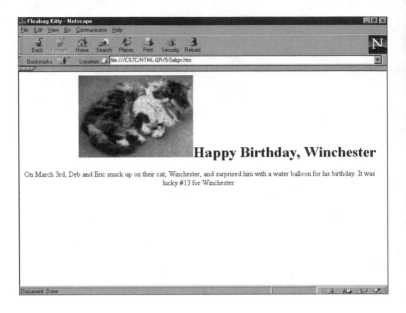

Using Type Specifications

As we mention in Part 1, "About HTML Basics," HTML was not designed to support specific formatting. Originally, HTML was conceived with the idea that authors would specify headings and lists while the reader (or the reader's browser) would take care of applying fonts and sizes. A generation of designers accustomed to desktop publishing and being able to control every aspect of document design, however, sought out ways to control HTML design as well. In response, newer browsers and the newest HTML specification provide some tags specifically to format text precisely.

If you choose to use these formatting commands, remember that not all browsers support them. Additionally, specifying fonts, in particular, carries no guarantee that your readers have the correct fonts or can display exactly what you want them to see. The following table shows the tags and attributes used to specify type characteristics.

HTML Tag or Attribute	Effect	Use in Pairs?
`<FONT>. . .</FONT>`	Changes the font.	Yes
`COLOR="#rrggbb"`	Colors the text based on the `rrggbb` number.	No
`FACE=". . ."`	Sets the typeface `NAME`. A list of font names can be specified.	No

HTML Tag or Attribute	Effect	Use in Pairs?
SIZE=n	Changes the font size n on a scale from 1 to 7.	No

Note: Before you begin, make sure that you have your browser and text editor open.

To change the characteristics of a specific block of text in the water balloons example, follow these steps:

1. Start your HTML document, which should look something like the following example:

```
<!DOCTYPE HTML PUBLIC "-//W3C//DTD HTML 3.2
  Final//EN">
<HTML>
<HEAD><TITLE>Making Effective Water Balloons
  </TITLE>
</HEAD>
<BODY>
<H1>Making Effective Water Balloons</H1>
<P>
Making water balloons is <EM>easy</EM> . . .
  but making <B>effective</B> water balloons
  takes time and patience. The result is a
  water balloon that does not break in your
  hand, offers <I>maximum splashing power
  </I>, and requires virtually no post-splat
  clean up.
</P>
</BODY>
</HTML>
```

2. Add the <FONT> tags around the text you want to change, as follows:

```
<H1>Making Effective Water Balloons</H1>
<P>
<FONT>
Making water balloons is <EM>easy</EM> . . .
  but making <B>effective</B> water balloons
  takes time and patience. The result is a
  water balloon that does not break in your
  hand, offers <I>maximum splashing power
  </I>, and requires virtually no post-splat
  clean up.
</FONT>
</P>
```

3. To change the size, add the appropriate SIZE= attribute to the font tag, as shown in the following example.

By default, the size is 4. (The number does not represent anything — it just is.) You can specify a size relative to the default (+1 for one size larger or –2 for two sizes smaller) or in absolute numbers such as 1 or 7.

```
<FONT SIZE=+2>
Making water balloons is <EM>easy</EM> . . .
    but making <B>effective</B> water balloons
    takes time and patience. The result is a
    water balloon that does not break in your
    hand, offers <I>maximum splashing power
    </I>, and requires virtually no post-splat
    clean up.
</FONT>
```

The following figure shows the results of the changed font size in a Web browser.

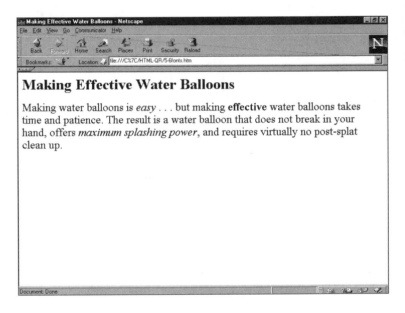

4. To change the typeface, add the FACE= attribute, as the following example shows.

You can name any font on your system (bearing in mind that the font also must be available on your reader's system to appear correctly). You can also list fonts in descending order of preference. If the first isn't available, your reader's browser moves along to the next and next.

```
<FONT FACE="Gill Sans, Courier, Arial" SIZE=+2>
Making water balloons is <EM>easy</EM> . . .
    but making <B>effective</B> water balloons
```

```
takes time and patience. The result is a
water balloon that does not break in your
hand, offers <I>maximum splashing power
</I>, and requires virtually no post-splat
clean up.
</FONT>
```

The following figure shows the new typeface in a Web browser.

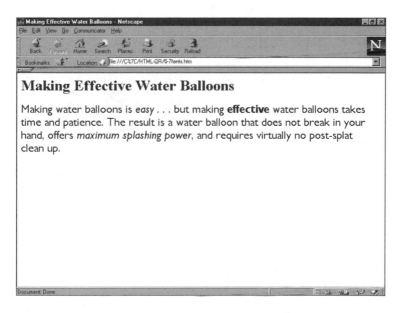

Reliable fonts for Windows include Arial, Times New Roman, and Courier New. Helvetica and Times are similar to Arial and Times New Roman and also are frequently available.

5. To change the color, add the COLOR= attribute, as shown in the following example.

As with other text color settings (described earlier in this part), you use an #rrggbb number to specify the color.

```
<FONT FACE="Gill Sans, Courier, Arial"
  COLOR=#ffffff SIZE=+2>
Making water balloons is <EM>easy</EM> . . .
  but making <B>effective</B> water balloons
  takes time and patience. The result is a
  water balloon that does not break in your
  hand, offers <I>maximum splashing power
  </I>, and requires virtually no post-splat
  clean up.
</FONT>
```

Breaking Lines

HTML allows you to break lines of text so that you can determine exactly (or as much as possible) how they appear on the users' end.

The following table shows the tag used to force line breaks.

HTML Tag	Effect	Use in Pairs?
` `	Breaks line; new line begins after tag.	No
`CLEAR=". . ."`	Requires that LEFT, RIGHT, or ALL margins are clear before new line starts.	No

To break lines of text so that each line appears the way you want it to (for example, in a poem), use the `<BR>` tag.

Note: Before beginning, make sure that you have your browser and text editor open and ready to create a new document. Or you can apply this information to an existing document.

Follow these steps:

1. Start your HTML page, which should look something like the following example:

```
<!DOCTYPE HTML PUBLIC "-//W3C//DTD HTML 3.2
   Final//EN">
<HTML>
<HEAD><TITLE>Ode to Food</TITLE></HEAD>
<BODY>

</BODY>
</HTML>
```

2. Type the information you want to include, with `<BR>` at the end of each line, as follows.

```
<P>
I'm Hungry, I'm Hungry! I said with a sigh,<BR>
I want to cancel dinner and go straight to my
   pie.<BR>
I want cake and ice cream and toast with
   jelly,<BR>
And I don't care if I grow a big belly.<BR>
</P>
```

If you are including a line break and want to make sure that the new line doesn't start until below an image, for example, you should add the `CLEAR=ALL` attribute to the `<BR>` tag. That forces the new line below all other objects on the line.

The following figure shows the effects of these line breaks.

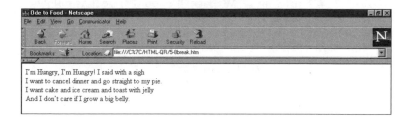

Including Horizontal Rules

HTML allows you to break up Web pages by applying a *horizontal rule,* `<HR>`. This horizontal rule can serve not only as a visual break for long pages but also as an informational break. The following table illustrates the tag used to create horizontal rules.

HTML Tag	Effect	Use in Pairs?
`<HR>`	Applies a horizontal rule.	No

You can change how the horizontal rule looks by using the attributes described in the following table.

HTML Attribute	Effect	Use in Pairs?
`SIZE=number`	Indicates how fat the rule is.	No
`WIDTH=number or percent"%"`	Specifies an exact width in pixels or percent of document width. A percentage value must appear in quotes, like `WIDTH="50%"`	No
`ALIGN=LEFT, CENTER, or RIGHT`	Specifies the alignment; works only in combination with `WIDTH`.	No

To use horizontal rules, apply the following tags and attributes.

Note: Before beginning, make sure that you have your browser and text editor open and ready to create a new document. Or you can apply this information to an existing document.

Follow these steps:

1. Start your HTML page; it should appear as follows:

```
<!DOCTYPE HTML PUBLIC "-//W3C//DTD HTML 3.2
    Final//EN">
<HTML>
<HEAD><TITLE>Lost Cat!</TITLE></HEAD>
<BODY>

</BODY>
</HTML>
```

2. Enter the text between the `<BODY>` tags and put in a few horizontal rules, as shown in this example:

```
<P><EM><H1 ALIGN=CENTER>Lost Cat!</H1></EM></P>
<HR WIDTH=80% ALIGN=CENTER>
<HR WIDTH=60% ALIGN=CENTER>
<HR WIDTH=40% ALIGN=CENTER>
<P>Fuzzy tortoise shell Persian — lost in Big
    Lake area. Probably looks confused.</P>
<HR>
<P>Answers to:
<UL>
<LI>Winchester
<LI>Hairheimer
<LI>Fritter
<LI>Sound of can opener
</UL></P>
<P>Please call if you find him: 555-9999</P>
<HR WIDTH=200>
<HR WIDTH=400>
<HR WIDTH=200>
<P ALIGN=RIGHT><I>Thanks!</I></P>
```

The following figure shows the effects of these tags.

```
Lost Cat! - Netscape                                                    _ B X
File  Edit  View  Go  Communicator  Help
  Back   Forward  Home  Search  Places  Print  Security  Reload          N

                              Lost Cat!


    ═══════════════════════════════════════════════════════════
        ═══════════════════════════════════════════════════
            ═══════════════════════════════════════════

    Fuzzy tortoise shell Persian — lost in Big Lake area. Probably looks confused.

    ───────────────────────────────────────────────────────────────

    Answers to:

        • Winchester
        • Hairheimer
        • Fritter
        • Sound of can opener

    Please call if you find him: 555-9999


                    ═══════════════════════════════
                ═══════════════════════════════════════
                    ═══════════════════════════════

                                                              Thanks!
 Document: Done
```

Getting carried away using horizontal rules, just as we did in this example, is not at all difficult. Our use of them here is definitely excessive. You should do as we say (not as we do) and use these rules only where they help readers find information more easily or help them wade through long passages of information.

Experiment with the SIZE, WIDTH, and ALIGN attributes. (The numbers used in the example are just that — examples of what you can do.) You can make the horizontal rules thinner, thicker, longer, or shorter, depending on the effect you want to achieve.

Making Tables

If you're pretty sure that everyone reading your HTML pages is going to be using a fairly new browser (less than two years old), you can use tables in your document. (Really old browsers can't handle this stuff.) Tables are very handy for the following purposes:

✦ Lining up material vertically and horizontally

✦ Making creative layouts

✦ Placing text beside graphics

The following table shows the tags and attributes used to create tables.

HTML Tag or Attribute	Effect	Use in Pairs?
`<TABLE>. . .</TABLE>`	Indicates table format.	Yes
`BORDER=n`	Controls table border width in pixels. 0 specifies no border.	No
`<TD>. . .</TD>`	Indicates table data cell.	Yes
`<TH>. . .</TH>`	Indicates table headings.	Yes
`<TR>. . .</TR>`	Indicates table row items.	Yes

This example shows you how to create a table with a couple of rows and columns.

Note: Before beginning, make sure that you have your browser and text editor open and ready to create a new document. Or you can apply this information to an existing document.

Our objective is a table containing the following information:

Culprit	Water Balloon Skills
Deborah	Fair
Eric	Excellent

To create a table with a couple of rows and a couple of columns, follow these steps.

1. Type your text, row by row, using a space or two between row elements, as follows:

```
Culprit Water Balloon Skills
Deborah Fair
Eric Excellent
```

2. Insert `<TABLE>` tags before and after the text to indicate the `<TABLE>` information that goes in the table, as shown here:

```
Culprit Water Balloon Skills
Deborah Fair
Eric Excellent
</TABLE>
```

3. Add `<TR>` tags to show where the table rows go, as the following example shows.

(***Remember:*** Rows go across the page.)

```
<TABLE>
<TR>Culprit Water Balloon Skills</TR>
<TR>Deborah Fair</TR>
<TR>Eric Excellent</TR>
</TABLE>
```

4. Add pairs of ⟨TH⟩ tags to show where the table heading cells go (in the top row), as follows.

At this point, adding some spacing may help you more easily see what's going on.

```
<TABLE>
<TR>
<TH>Culprit</TH>
<TH>Water Balloon Skills</TH>
</TR>
<TR>Deborah Fair</TR>
<TR>Eric Excellent</TR>
</TABLE>
```

5. Add pairs of ⟨TD⟩ tags to indicate the individual cells of a table, as shown here:

```
<TABLE>
<TR><TH>Culprit</TH>
<TH>Water Balloon Skills</TH>
</TR>
<TR><TD>Deborah</TD> <TD>Fair</TD></TR>
<TR><TD>Eric</TD> <TD>Excellent</TD></TR>
</TABLE>
```

6. Add the BORDER attribute to the ⟨TABLE⟩ tag to create lines around each table cell, as the following example shows:

```
<TABLE BORDER=1>
<TR><TH>Culprit</TH>
<TH>Water Balloon Skills</TH>
</TR>
<TR><TD>Deborah </TD> <TD>Fair</TD></TR>
<TR><TD>Eric </TD> <TD>Excellent</TD></TR>
</TABLE>
```

The following figure shows the results of all this work.

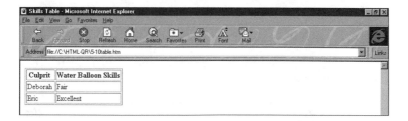

You can be creative with table borders if you want. You can, for example, create a table without borders — just don't include the BORDER=1 attribute in the ⟨TABLE⟩ tag. You should take this action if the table appears cluttered with many rows or columns or if you're using the table as a formatting tool (for example, if you want to include text next to a graphic). You can also increase the thickness of the border by increasing the number to the attribute: BORDER=5.

Experiment with tables. You can come up with many creative layouts and page designs. Here are some ideas:

✦ Embed images in tables (to align graphics and text the way you want).

✦ Place links within tables.

✦ Place headings to the left (or right) of a paragraph of text.

If you find that your tables have problems — or don't seem to work at all — make very sure that your tags are paired correctly and that you haven't omitted any tags. Printing out the source and marking off pairs of tags is sometimes necessary for troubleshooting tables. As you can see from the very small example in the text, getting confused is very easy with all the different tags necessary to use for tables. Additionally, you can save yourself some trouble by liberally using white space and blank lines as you create the table. That extra white space can help you see what's going on.

Providing Author and Contact Information

Good Web pages provide information about the author or about how to contact the author. The first corollary to that statement is that good Web page authors (such as yourself) include their contact information in their pages. As a result, users can follow up or obtain information not included on the Web site.

You can provide such information by doing one (or both) of two things:

✦ Use an address tag

✦ Use a return e-mail hyperlink

The following table shows a tag and a URL used to provide contact information.

HTML Tag or URL	Effect	Use in Pairs?
`<ADDRESS>. . . </ADDRESS>`	Indicates address or contact information; generally appears in italics.	Yes
`MAILTO:yourid@your. email.address`	Indicates a specific e-mail address for use with HREF="..."	No

Using an address tag

Using an address is handy for indicating authors, including contact information, and including any other notices, warnings, or copyrights. An address tag also helps users roaming the Internet seeking good Web pages to spot your address quickly!

Note: Before beginning, make sure that you have your browser and text editor open.

To use an address, just add the information near the bottom of your Web page, as shown in the following example.

```
<!DOCTYPE HTML PUBLIC "-//W3C//DTD HTML 3.2
   Final//EN">
<HTML>
<HEAD><TITLE>Winchester's Resume</TITLE></HEAD>
<BODY>
<H1 ALIGN=CENTER>Winchester's Resume</H1>
<P>
<UL>
<LI>I sleep.
<LI>I eat.
<LI>I cough up hairballs.
</UL>
</P>
<ADDRESS>Information provided by Deb and Eric
   Ray<BR>
(Winchester's Reluctant Owners)<BR>
Tulsa, OK 74114<BR>
(555) 222-1111<BR>
</ADDRESS>
</BODY>
</HTML>
```

The following figure shows the effects of this addition.

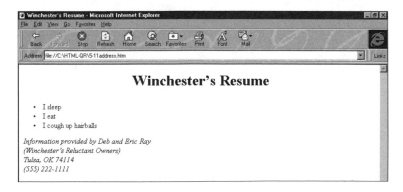

Using an e-mail return

To provide really complete contact information, you can use an e-mail link that allows users to e-mail directly from the Web site.

To use an e-mail return just add a link to the names in the identification section. Use the following URL (edited appropriately to show your real e-mail address):

```
mailto:your-email@your.address.com
```

Note: Before beginning, make sure that you have your browser and text editor open.

See also Part III, specifically the section called "Making Basic Links" (especially if you read the section heading three times and still don't understand it).

```
<ADDRESS>Information provided by
<A HREF="mailto:authors@raycomm.com">Deb and Eric
Ray</A><BR>
(Winchester's Reluctant Owners)<BR>
Tulsa, OK 74114<BR>
(555) 222-1111<BR>
</ADDRESS>
</BODY>
</HTML>
```

The following figure shows the new hyperlink in your document.

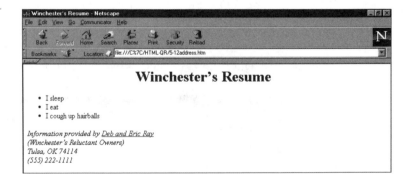

Part VI

Serving HTML to the World

In Part VI, we introduce you to the task of placing your HTML documents on a server so that potentially anyone connected to the Internet can see your documents. Although this part gets a little technical in places, we assure you that it's not that bad. We also walk you through the use of some of the neat additional capabilities that an HTML server gives you.

In several places, we insert an "Ask for Help" icon and direct you to your Web server administrator (or Webmaster) to find out how your Web server is organized and what is available for your use. Don't hesitate to get to know your server administrators. They can give you all kinds of useful information about the server and what's special about the way it's set up.

See also Part II for information about tags if you need a quick brush-up on using them. In this part, we don't address tag basics — we just tell you to apply them.

In this part . . .

- 🖙 **Learning about servers**
- 🖙 **Determining your URL**
- 🖙 **Finding out about server programs**
- 🖙 **Including files or information automatically**
- 🖙 **Placing material on a server**
- 🖙 **Creating forms**

About Servers

Servers (also known as *HTML servers, http servers,* or *Web servers*) send HTML documents to any computer on the network that requests them. In most cases, servers are located on the Internet and serve documents to any other computer on the Net.

Sometimes servers are located on a corporate *intranet* and are accessible only from other computers in that corporation. No matter whether you're producing HTML pages for publication on the Internet or on a corporate intranet, you need to complete the following steps:

1. Prepare your documents.

2. Put them on the server.

3. Test the documents.

4. Enhance them with any server-specific capabilities (such as the ones we talk about in this part).

5. Put the documents on the server again.

6. Test them again (and feel free to repeat this step as often as you want).

As a rule of thumb, don't put anything on a server that you're not prepared for the entire world to see. Even if you don't think that people can see your handiwork (for example, because you don't have any links into that document), little information-seeking programs roam the Internet, and they can find it — particularly if they shouldn't.

Any computer on the network, even that PC on your desktop, can function as a Web server. Just how to set up Web servers is way beyond the scope of this book, but if your computer is always on and always connected to the Internet, you can make it a Web server.

Web servers don't necessarily have anything to do with local area network (LAN) servers. *See also* Part I for information about LANs.

Check out *HTML For Dummies,* 2nd Edition, by Ed Tittel and Steve James (published by IDG Books Worldwide, Inc.), for more information about setting up Web servers.

Determining Your URL

Your server has a specific name. It's probably something like www.company.com or www.organization.org, which means

that the basic URL for pages on that server is `http://
www.organization.org/` or `http://www.company.com/`. Your
server administrator probably gives you a directory or set of
directories in which you put all the documents that you want to
serve to the world.

You can obtain your URL from the Web administrator or possibly
by reading documentation about your Web site. Don't bank on the
documentation, however — Web servers are much too often
poorly documented, and you may find that asking your administrator is easier than trying to find the answer yourself.

In all likelihood, if you have an account with an Internet Service
Provider (ISP) your base URL ends up as `http://
www.organization.com/~yourid/`, just as ours is `http://
www.xmission.com/~ejray/`. Obviously, in the place of `yourid`,
you have a real ID, which you use to sign onto the system. You can
place all of the documents that you develop on the server in your
account. Their absolute URLs start with your base URL and
include all additional file or directory information.

See also Part III for a review of URLs and files.

If you're paying big bucks for your Web site or if you're the
Webmaster for your (probably somewhat large) organization, you
may have a URL such as `http://www.mysite.com/`, with
`mysite` being your actual business. If you want to have your
organization name appear in the server name, ask your administrator about *virtual domains,* which give you the glory of your own
name without the hassle of needing to maintain the server. The
same information about putting your HTML documents on the
server applies, but, remember that going this way makes you look
more expensive.

If you're the new Webmaster for your organization, good for you!
The job's fun. (Really!) If that's your situation and we tell you to
see your Webmaster for help, just find the server administrator or
the head geek in your organization.

Getting Documents onto the Server

Every time you make changes or updates to your documents, you
must put those changes back on the server so your readers can
see them. Just as you've become used to making your changes in
your document, saving it, and then clicking the reload key, you
find a pattern to making changes to a document on the server. We
suggest performing the following steps:

1. Make your changes.

2. Save your changes.

3. Upload your changes to the server.

4. Reload your browser to check out the changes.

 How, you ask, do I get my documents on the server? You most likely use an *FTP* (file transfer protocol) program to put your documents on the server. Your server administrator can fill you in on the procedure. You may want to use WS-FTP (for Windows), Fetch (for Macintosh), or some form of plain FTP (mostly for UNIX) to transfer your files to the server. Many Web-authoring packages now also provide built-in file-transfer capabilities — check out Netscape Gold or Netscape Composer on all platforms, as well as Microsoft's Web Publishing Wizard if you're a Windows 95 user.

See also Part I for information about FTP programs.

Getting Server Programs

Server programs are small additions to the actual Web server that allow you to do cool stuff. They're basically the things that differentiate between what you can do on your own computer and what you can do on the server. Finding out about server programs is pretty much a "see your server administrator" task.

An example of these programs are the little counters (which we discuss in the section "Including a Counter," later in this part) that record how many times people access your Web page. You can include a line in your HTML to tell the server to run the program, add one to the count, and display the total in your page. These programs, however, are sometimes a bit difficult to access.

 You've probably noticed that server administrators are pretty tense about security (and justifiably so). Generally, you find very few directories on a server in which you can run a program for your Web pages. But if your administrator permits you to run a server program, such as the counter dealie we just mentioned, she must put that program in the right place on the system, such as the `cgi-bin` directory, which is where server programs traditionally live.

If you're doing your Web pages on a budget or if your server administrator is fairly busy, using existing programs is probably the only alternative. To find out what programs are available, you may ask your administrator the following questions:

✦ What programs are available in the `cgi-bin` (pronounced see-gee-eye-bin) directory?

+ What do these programs do?

+ How do I find their instructions?

+ Whom do I call if the programs don't work?

Linking Things Automatically

One time-saving tip is to automatically include information within your HTML documents. Just as many e-mail programs automatically affix a signature to the end of the message, you can have your HTML pages automatically include other documents.

Your server administrator must enable *server-side includes* before automatic links to information can work. A server-side include is a command that tells the server to include other information with the document being served.

These includes do have a downside — they slow the server somewhat. On the other hand, if you're inserting many graphics, your readers aren't going to notice the difference that a small include makes.

Some servers require that files with server-side includes have an extension of .shtml, rather than .html. This extension just helps the server know what's going on. Your server administrator can tell you whether this extension is necessary.

You can include many goodies. We recommend, however, that you stick to a couple of useful basics — the date and the time that the document was last modified. Other information, such as the address of the computer receiving (not serving) the document, is possible but tends to be pretty pretentious. The following table shows some of the tags and attributes that can be included from many servers.

HTML Tag or Attribute	Effect	Use in Pairs?
`<! -. . .- >`	Indicates a comment or server command.	No
`#INCLUDE`	Indicates to include a file.	No
`FILE=". . ."`	Indicates the filename relative to the directory.	No
`VIRTUAL=". . ."`	Indicates the filename relative to the server.	No
`#ECHO VAR=". . ."`	Indicates to display the value of a variable.	No

(continued)

HTML Tag or Attribute	Effect	Use in Pairs?
DATE_LOCAL	Indicates that the variable to display is the local date.	No
LAST_MODIFIED	Indicates that the variable to display is the last time the document was changed.	No

If, for example, your company is prone to takeovers and you fear that you may spend the next three years changing and rechanging the company name in all your Web pages, you can automate the process so that you need to make a change only once; it then shows up in all your pages. Use the following steps to perform that task:

1. Create a new HTML document that contains the name of the company.

In this document, do *not* use the ⟨HEAD⟩, ⟨BODY⟩, or ⟨HTML⟩ tags — just type the name of the company.

2. Enter ⟨!--#include file="companyname.html"--⟩ in every other document where you want to include the company name.

3. Upload both the documents — one with the company name, one (or more) with the cryptic command — to the server.

You should find the company name right where it belongs in the second file. (If you view your document from your computer, you can't see anything in this place.)

The cool part is that you can go back and change the companyname.html file to reflect the new name, and you're back in business. You can include a file in as many other documents as you want. Granted, using just the company name isn't that impressive, but if you take these steps with all information you repeat verbatim on several pages, you're going to be in great shape. Think of what you can do with the company name, address, phone number, president's name, and so on.

Including a Counter

As we mentioned earlier, a *counter* is that little feature that tells you how many people have visited an HTML document. Keep in mind that it's a mixed bag — sometimes you may not want everyone to know how many (or few) people visit your pages.

This example shows you how to include a counter in your Web page.

Note: Before you add a counter, you must have an existing HTML document to which to add the counter. We assume that your document is ready to go.

Your server administrator can tell you the exact format to use to place a counter in your document. Our administrator said that the magic phrase is `<!--#exec cgi="/cgi-bin/counter"-->`.

To include a counter in your Web page, follow these basic steps:

1. Start with a basic HTML document, similar to the following:

```
<HTML>
<HEAD><TITLE>Lucy Counts, Too</TITLE></HEAD>
<BODY>
<H1>Lucy Counts, Too</H1>
<P>This page is dedicated to Lucy, who is less
   gross and more cute than Winchester. <B>
   people have visited this page.</B></P>
</BODY>
</HTML>
```

2. Add the counter tag at the place where you want the number, as follows.

(Make sure that you leave a space on each side so that the counter doesn't run into the text.)

```
<HTML>
<HEAD><TITLE>Lucy Counts, Too</TITLE></HEAD>
<BODY>
<H1>Lucy Counts, Too</H1>
<P>This page is dedicated to Lucy, who is less
   gross and more cute than Winchester. <B>
   <!--#exec cgi="/cgi-bin/counter"--> people
   have visited this page.</B></P>
</BODY>
</HTML>
```

3. Save and then upload your document to the server and check it out.

You then see something similar to the following figure.

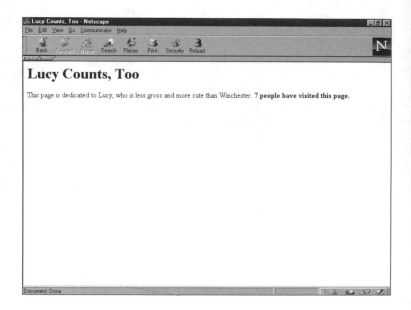

Producing Forms

In HTML, *forms* are just what they are in real life — a fairly imper-
sonal, pretty effective means of getting standardized information
from other people. You may use forms to facilitate the following
tasks:

+ Conduct a survey

+ Collect addresses or information about visitors to your HTML
  pages

+ Allow people to register for something

Notice that in creating forms, you need to make sure that the
information gets back to you. To do so, you must check with your
server administrator to find out exactly what you need to do to get
the information e-mailed to you. The following table shows the
basic <FORM> tags and attributes you use.

HTML Tag or Attribute	Effect	Use in Pairs?
`<FORM. . .>` `</FORM>`	Encloses the entire form.	Yes
`ACTION=". . ."`	Identifies what should happen to the data after the form is submitted.	No

HTML Tag or Attribute	Effect	Use in Pairs?
ENCTYPE=". . ."	Identifies MIME type of form data.	No
METHOD=". . ."	Identifies methods; valid options are GET or POST — one is required.	No

The basic <FORM> tag is a two-parter, having both an initial tag and a closing tag. You can use the <FORM> tag to have information sent back to you directly or to a program that compiles the information for you.

The basic <FORM> tag has two attributes, and your server administrator can provide you with each of them. Tell your administrator that you want to create a form that can be e-mailed to your personal address — the administrator can tell you what to fill in.

Suppose your administrator tells you to use the following elements:

```
ACTION="http://www.xmission.com/cgi-bin/
    email?raycomm"METHOD=POST
```

Notice that the rest of our examples are constructed based on this information. Just ask your server administrator exactly what to use (or where to look for instructions).

This example shows you how to include a form in your Web page.

Note: Before you jump into creating a form, you must have an existing HTML document to add the form to. We assume that the following information is true:

✦ You've already gotten the information that you need from your administrator.

✦ You have your HTML document open in an editing program.

✦ You've opened the HTML document in your browser so that you can view and test the document.

✦ You completely understand that we *never* do *anything* to hurt cats.

To include a form in your Web page, follow these basic steps:

1. Start with a basic HTML document, similar to this one:

```
<!DOCTYPE HTML PUBLIC "-//W3C//DTD HTML 3.2
    Final//EN">
<HTML>
<HEAD><TITLE>Survey: How to Get the Cats
    </TITLE></HEAD>
```

```
<BODY>
<H1>Survey: How to Get the Cats</H1>
<P>We've decided to take a survey about the
    best pranks to play on the cats.Please
    complete the survey and click the Submit
    button.</P>
</BODY>
</HTML>
```

2. Add the `<FORM>` and `</FORM>` tags to show where the form goes, as follows:

```
Please complete the survey and click the Submit
    button.</P>
<FORM>
</FORM>
</BODY>
</HTML>
```

3. Add the information that your server administrator gave you for the link, as shown here:

```
<FORM METHOD="POST"
ACTION="http://www.xmission.com/cgi-bin/
    email?raycomm">
</FORM>
```

The following figure shows the basic document.

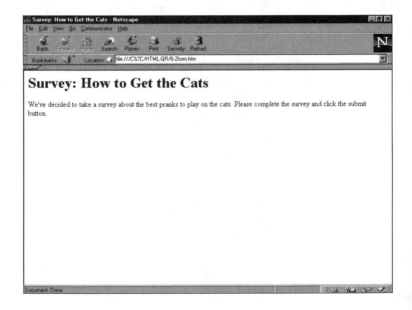

At this point, you can't see anything different about your page. Nor can you test the page out to find out whether it works. Just forge ahead and finish up the form and you can satisfy your curiosity.

 Your server administrator most likely gives you an `ACTION` attribute that mails the results of the form back to you. Even if you find someone who wants to write a program to automatically collect all the responses to your HTML form, your form doesn't change — you just need to change the `ACTION` attribute after (or if) the programmer finishes that project.

About form tags

If you have the basics of the form under control, you now want to include some `<INPUT>` fields so that you can start collecting information. The form-input tags shown in the following table, in many permutations, should carry you through the next several sections.

HTML Tag or Attribute	Effect	Use in Pairs?
`<INPUT. . .>`	Identifies some type of input field.	No
`CHECKED`	Shows which item is selected by default (checkbox/radio button).	No
`MAXLENGTH=n`	Indicates the maximum number of characters in the field width.	No
`NAME=". . ."`	Indicates the name of the field.	No
`SIZE=n`	Displays field n characters wide.	
`TYPE=". . ."`	Indicates the type of field. Valid types are `TEXT`, `PASSWORD`, `CHECKBOX`, `RADIO`, `SUBMIT`, `RESET`, `FILE`, `IMAGE`, and `HIDDEN`.	No
`VALUE=". . ."`	Indicates value of button (and the label for Submit and Reset).	No

Using Input and Reset buttons

Now that you've created the form, you need to add *Submit* and *Reset* buttons that the users click to submit the form (or start over again if they goofed up). The Submit button sends the information in after your readers click it, while the Reset button just clears the input from the form.

 To include Submit and Reset buttons, enter the following text and tags in your HTML document.

Note: You need a functional form before you start adding Submit and Reset buttons.

```
<FORM METHOD="POST" ACTION="http://
    www.xmission.com/cgi-bin/email?raycomm">
<INPUT TYPE="SUBMIT" VALUE="Submit">
<INPUT TYPE="RESET" VALUE="Reset">
</FORM>
</BODY>
</HTML>
```

The following figure shows these two buttons in your HTML document.

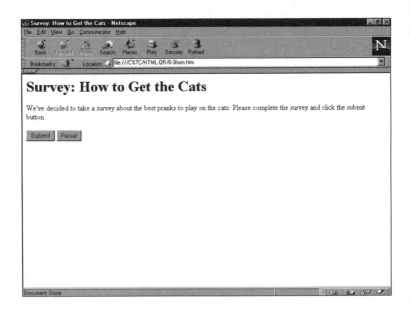

The VALUE= attributes determine what text appears on the buttons. You can change the VALUE of the TYPE="RESET" button to "Forget it!" The full tag then looks as follows:

```
<INPUT TYPE="RESET" VALUE="Forget it!">
```

Using checkboxes, radio buttons, and more

Checkboxes and *radio buttons* are the objects that users can click to select choices from a list. Checkboxes allow you to select multiple options. Radio buttons are designed so that you can choose one from a list — just like with pushing buttons on a car radio. Both checkboxes and radio buttons are variations on the INPUT field. The following figure shows examples of both.

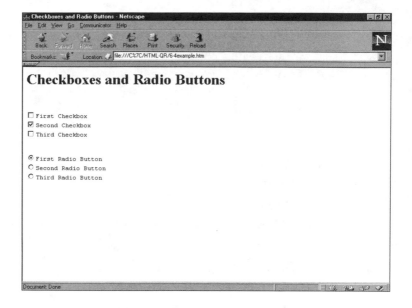

Making checkboxes

Making checkboxes is not complicated — you use several tags, but the process is the same as creating anything else by using HTML.

This example shows you how to use checkboxes in your document.

Note: You need to have a functional form, including Submit and Reset buttons, before you add checkboxes. You start with the following example — just a section of a complete document — and build on it. (And *remember* — we dearly love our cats and really wouldn't ever surprise them with a balloon — water or otherwise.)

```
<FORM METHOD="POST" ACTION="http://
    www.xmission.com/cgi-bin/email?raycomm">
<INPUT TYPE="SUBMIT" VALUE="Submit">
<INPUT TYPE="RESET" VALUE="Reset">
</FORM>
```

To use checkboxes in your document, follow these steps:

1. Enter an `<INPUT>` tag on the blank line after the beginning of the form, as follows:

```
<FORM METHOD="POST" ACTION="http://
    www.xmission.com/cgi-bin/email?raycomm">
<INPUT>
<INPUT TYPE="SUBMIT" VALUE="Submit">
<INPUT TYPE="RESET"VALUE="Reset">
</FORM>
```

2. Identify the type that you want to use, as shown in the following example.

(We start with a checkbox.)

```
<FORM METHOD="POST" ACTION="http://
   www.xmission.com/cgi-bin/email?raycomm">
<INPUT TYPE="CHECKBOX">
<INPUT TYPE="SUBMIT" VALUE="Submit">
<INPUT TYPE="RESET" VALUE="Reset">
</FORM>
```

3. Insert the text that you want people to see behind that checkbox, as follows.

(Until you do so, they see a checkbox with no description.)

```
<FORM METHOD="POST" ACTION="http://
   www.xmission.com/cgi-bin/email?raycomm">
<INPUT TYPE="CHECKBOX">Throw a balloon!
<INPUT TYPE="SUBMIT" VALUE="Submit">
<INPUT TYPE="RESET" VALUE="Reset">
</FORM>
```

4. Identify the name of the INPUT field, as shown here.

(You see this field as you're reading the input from your form. Make the name something short and logical.)

```
<FORM METHOD="POST" ACTION="http://
   www.xmission.com/cgi-bin/email?raycomm">
<INPUT TYPE="CHECKBOX" NAME="Throw"> Throw a
   balloon!
<INPUT TYPE="SUBMIT" VALUE="Submit">
<INPUT TYPE="RESET" VALUE="Reset">
</FORM>
```

5. Enter the text that you want to see if someone selects this option, as shown in the following example.

Remember: Whenever you see the output of this form, it's probably as an e-mail message with just words in the place of the pretty check marks, so you can't look at the checks. We recommend something similar to the NAME attribute. Make this one short and to the point.

```
<FORM METHOD="POST"  ACTION="http://
   www.xmission.com/cgi-bin/email?raycomm">
<INPUT TYPE="CHECKBOX" NAME="Throw"
   VALUE="ThrowBalloon"> Throw a balloon!
<INPUT TYPE="SUBMIT" VALUE="Submit">
<INPUT TYPE="RESET" VALUE="Reset">
</FORM>
```

6. Enter a couple more lines to complete the list, as follows (because you probably don't want a checkbox list with only one thing to check).

(We also added a `<P>` tag at the end to force a new line.)

```
<FORM METHOD="POST" ACTION="http://
    www.xmission.com/cgi-bin/email?raycomm">
<INPUT TYPE="CHECKBOX" NAME="Throw"
    VALUE="ThrowBalloon"> Throw a balloon!
<INPUT TYPE="CHECKBOX" NAME="Hurl"
    VALUE="HurlBalloon"> Hurl a balloon!
<INPUT TYPE="CHECKBOX" NAME="Lob"
    VALUE="LobBalloon"> Lob a balloon!<P>
<INPUT TYPE="SUBMIT" VALUE="Submit">
<INPUT TYPE="RESET" VALUE="Reset">
</FORM>
```

7. Enter a `CHECKED` attribute in the checkbox that you want to have selected by default, as in the following example.

(Do so if you want to select a checkbox in advance to give a recommendation or to make sure that something gets checked.)

```
<FORM METHOD="POST" ACTION="http://
    www.xmission.com/cgi-bin/email?raycomm">
<INPUT TYPE="CHECKBOX" NAME="Throw"
    VALUE="ThrowBalloon"> Throw a balloon!
<INPUT CHECKED TYPE="CHECKBOX" NAME="Hurl"
    VALUE="HurlBalloon"> Hurl a balloon!
<INPUT TYPE="CHECKBOX" NAME="Lob"
    VALUE="LobBalloon"> Lob a balloon!
<INPUT TYPE="SUBMIT" VALUE="Submit">
<INPUT TYPE="RESET" VALUE="Reset">
</FORM>
```

The following figure shows the form with the addition of checkboxes.

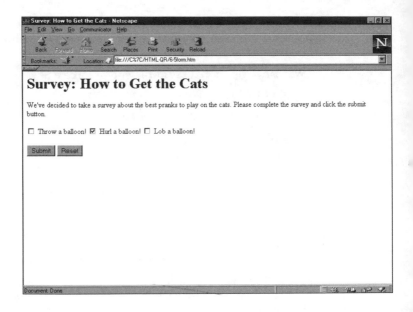

Making radio buttons

Making radio buttons is similar to making checkboxes — you use several tags, and the process is the same as that for using other HTML tags.

This example shows you how to include radio buttons in your form.

Note: Before you start making radio buttons, make sure that you already have your functional form completed. This example uses the following form (developed in other examples in this chapter):

```
<FORM METHOD="POST" ACTION="http://
  www.xmission.com/cgi-bin/email?raycomm">
<INPUT TYPE="CHECKBOX" NAME="Throw"
  VALUE="ThrowBalloon"> Throw a balloon!
<INPUT CHECKED TYPE="CHECKBOX" NAME="Hurl"
  VALUE="HurlBalloon"> Hurl a balloon!
<INPUT TYPE="CHECKBOX" NAME="Lob"
  VALUE="LobBalloon"> Lob a balloon!
<INPUT TYPE="SUBMIT" VALUE="Submit">
<INPUT TYPE="RESET" VALUE="Reset">
</FORM>
```

To include radio buttons in your form, follow these steps:

1. Insert the `<INPUT>` tag and the text that people should see, as follows:

```
<INPUT>Do it--it'll be funny!
<INPUT TYPE="SUBMIT" VALUE="Submit">
<INPUT TYPE="RESET" VALUE="Reset">
</FORM>
```

2. Add the TYPE indicator to show that it is a radio button, as shown here:

```
<INPUT TYPE="RADIO">Do it--it'll be funny!
```

3. Add the NAME indicator, as follows.

(The NAME applies to the whole set of radio buttons, so we've chosen a less specific name.)

```
<INPUT TYPE="RADIO" NAME="Prank">Do it--it'll
    be funny!
```

4. Add the VALUE attribute, as in the following example.

(Again, this value is what you see after you get the input of the form back, so make this value unique to this choice and make it descriptive.)

```
<INPUT TYPE="RADIO" NAME="Prank" VALUE="Do">
    Do it--it'll be funny!
```

5. Add the CHECKED attribute again, as follows, because this selection is the recommended choice:

```
<INPUT TYPE="RADIO" NAME="Prank" VALUE="Do"
    CHECKED>Do it--it'll be funny!
```

6. Add as many more radio buttons to this set as you want, along with line breaks (
 or <P>) in between them just to make them look nice, as shown here.

(Remember that radio buttons are designed to accept only one selection from the group, so make sure that they all share the same NAME field. This way, the computer knows that they belong together.)

```
<INPUT TYPE="RADIO" NAME="Prank" VALUE="Do"
    CHECKED>Do it--it'll be funny!<BR>
<INPUT TYPE="RADIO" NAME="Prank"
    VALUE="DoNot">Don't play a prank, meanie!<BR>
<INPUT TYPE="RADIO" NAME="Prank"
    VALUE="DoNotCare">I couldn't care less.
    They're your cats, and you'll have to live
    with yourself.<P>
```

The following figure shows the addition of radio buttons to the form.

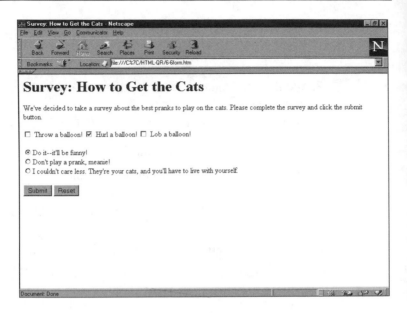

If you're testing your form and you find that the CHECKED attribute doesn't seem to be working, click the Reset button within your form. (If you're following along, remember that a previous example explained how to change the Reset button to say "Forget it.")

Using other input types

Other input types, such as TEXT, can be very useful. TEXT allows you to insert a small amount of information (such as a name or an address) into your form.

This example shows you how to include text-input areas in your form.

Note: Before you start adding other input attributes, make sure that you already have your functional form completed. This example uses the following form (developed in other examples in this chapter):

```
<FORM METHOD="POST"
ACTION="http://www.xmission.com/cgi-bin/
  email?raycomm">
<INPUT TYPE="CHECKBOX" NAME="Throw"
  VALUE="ThrowBalloon"> Throw a balloon!
<INPUT CHECKED TYPE="CHECKBOX" NAME="Hurl"
  VALUE="HurlBalloon"> Hurl a balloon!
<INPUT TYPE="CHECKBOX" NAME="Lob"
  VALUE="LobBalloon"> Lob a balloon!<P>
```

```
<INPUT TYPE="RADIO" NAME="Prank" VALUE="Do"
   CHECKED>Do it--it'll be funny!<BR>
<INPUT TYPE="RADIO" NAME="Prank"
   VALUE="DoNot">Don't play a prank, meanie!<BR>
<INPUT TYPE="RADIO" NAME="Prank"
   VALUE="DoNotCare">I couldn't care less.
   They're your cats, and you'll have to live
   with yourself.<P>
<INPUT TYPE="SUBMIT" VALUE="Submit">
<INPUT TYPE="RESET" VALUE="Reset">
</FORM>
```

You're going to add the input area to the form that you've been developing, so check the previous section for context, if necessary.

To include text-input areas in your form, follow these steps:

1. Insert the `<INPUT>` tag and the text that people should see, plus a tag (`<BR>` or `<P>`) to force a new line, as follows:

```
<INPUT>Your Name<P>
<INPUT TYPE="SUBMIT" VALUE="Submit">
<INPUT TYPE="RESET" VALUE="Reset">
</FORM>
```

2. Add the TYPE indicator to show that it is a text input area, as shown here:

```
<INPUT TYPE="TEXT">Your Name<P>
```

3. Add the NAME indicator, as follows:

```
<INPUT TYPE="TEXT" NAME="name">Your Name<P>
```

4. Add the SIZE indicator to tell the field how many characters wide it should be, as shown here:

```
<INPUT SIZE=35 TYPE="TEXT" NAME="name">Your
   Name<P>
```

The following figure shows the addition of the text input field to your form.

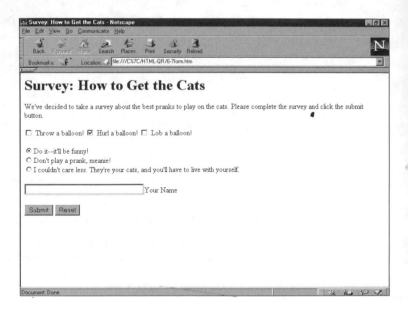

Other input types can also be pretty useful. You can, for example, insert a password-type field if you think your readers may want to make sure that their entry isn't visible to anyone. Just replace the TYPE=TEXT attribute with TYPE=PASSWORD.

If you develop many forms, you may also find useful having information submitted with the form that your readers don't see. You can include the purpose for the form, for example, as a VALUE so that it's sent back to you. You do so by adding a VALUE and changing the TYPE=TEXT attribute to TYPE=HIDDEN. The readers can't see the form field, but you can after you get the results of the form. Your code looks as follows: <INPUT NAME="note" VALUE="Nonsense" TYPE=HIDDEN>.

Using select lists

Select lists are lists from which your readers can choose one or more items. They're like the font selection drop-down list in your word processing program.

The following table shows the tags and attributes used to include select lists in your HTML document.

HTML Tag or Attribute	Effect	Use in Pairs?
<SELECT. . .> . . . </SELECT>	Provides a list of items to select.	Yes

HTML Tag or Attribute	Effect	Use in Pairs?
MULTIPLE	Indicates that multiple selections are allowed.	No
NAME=". . ."	Indicates the name of the field.	No
SIZE=n	Determines the size of the scrollable list by showing n options.	No
<OPTION. . .>	Precedes each item in an option list.	Yes
SELECTED	Identifies which option is selected by default.	No
VALUE=". . ."	Indicates the value of the field.	No

This example shows you how to add a select list to your form.

Note: Before including select lists, make sure that you already have a functional form completed. This example uses the following form (developed in other examples in this chapter):

```
<FORM METHOD="POST" ACTION="http://
    www.xmission.com/cgi-bin/email?raycomm">
<INPUT TYPE="CHECKBOX" NAME="Throw"
    VALUE="ThrowBalloon"> Throw a balloon!
<INPUT CHECKED TYPE="CHECKBOX" NAME="Hurl"
    VALUE="HurlBalloon"> Hurl a balloon!
<INPUT TYPE="CHECKBOX" NAME="Lob"
    VALUE="LobBalloon"> Lob a balloon!<P>
<INPUT TYPE="RADIO" NAME="Prank" VALUE="Do"
    CHECKED>Do it—it'll be funny!<BR>
<INPUT TYPE="RADIO" NAME="Prank"
    VALUE="DoNot">Don't play a prank, meanie!<BR>
<INPUT TYPE="RADIO" NAME="Prank"
    VALUE="DoNotCare">I couldn't care less. They're
    your cats, and you'll have to live with
    yourself.<P>
<INPUT SIZE=35 TYPE="TEXT" NAME="name">Your Name<P>
<INPUT TYPE="SUBMIT" VALUE="Submit">
<INPUT TYPE="RESET" VALUE="Reset">
</FORM>
```

To add a select list to your form, follow these steps:

1. Insert the <SELECT> tags into your document and a tag (
 or <P>) to force a new line, as follows:

```
<SELECT>
</SELECT><P>
<INPUT TYPE="SUBMIT" VALUE="Submit">
<INPUT TYPE="RESET" VALUE="Reset">
</FORM>
```

2. Add the `NAME` attribute to the `<SELECT>` tag, as shown here.

(The `NAME` should be appropriately broad to cover the spectrum of choices.)

```
<SELECT NAME="Method">
</SELECT><P>
```

3. Add an `<OPTION>` that your readers can select, as follows:

```
<SELECT NAME="Method">
<OPTION VALUE="single">Single Balloon
</SELECT><P>
```

4. Complete your `<SELECT>` section by adding the other possible choices, as shown in the following example:

```
<SELECT NAME="Method">
<OPTION VALUE="single">Single Balloon
<OPTION VALUE="multiple">Multiple Balloons
<OPTION VALUE="hose">Just Use the Hose
</SELECT><P>
```

The following figure shows the addition of the select list to your form.

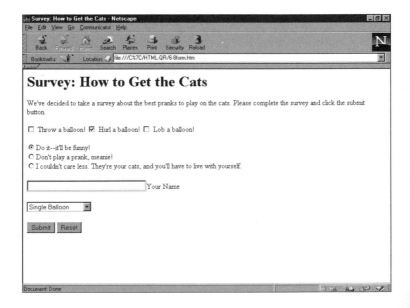

TIP

Don't underestimate the flexibility of your SELECT area. You can add a SIZE=3 attribute to the <SELECT> tag, for example, so that three items are visible at once. Your opening <SELECT> tag now looks as follows: <SELECT SIZE=3 NAME="Method">. Your result looks like the example in the following figure.

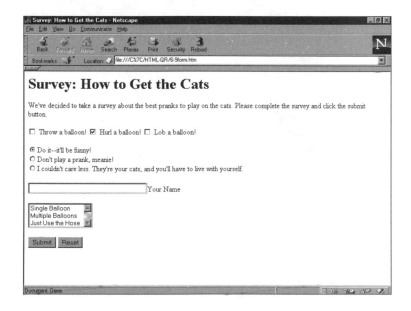

To allow people to select more than one item in your area, just add MULTIPLE to the opening <SELECT> tag. People can then click multiple items to make multiple selections as shown in the following figure.

Using *<TEXTAREA>* tags

Text areas are open spaces in your form in which your readers can type comments or enter other information.

The following table shows the tags and attributes used to add text areas to your form.

HTML Tag or Attribute	Effect	Use in Pairs?
`<TEXTAREA . . .>` `. . .</TEXTAREA>`	Encloses a multiline text field. The enclosed text is the value displayed in the field.	Yes
`COLS=n`	Indicates the number of columns in the field.	No
`NAME=". . ."`	Indicates the name of the field.	No
`ROWS=n`	Indicates the number of rows in the field.	No

This example shows you how to add a text area to your form.

Note: You need to have a functional form, including Input and Reset buttons, before you add `<TEXTAREA>` tags. We start with the following example — developed in other examples in this part — and build on it:

```
<FORM METHOD="POST"
ACTION="http://www.xmission.com/cgi-bin/
    email?raycomm">
```

```
<INPUT TYPE="CHECKBOX" NAME="Throw"
    VALUE="ThrowBalloon"> Throw a balloon!
<INPUT CHECKED TYPE="CHECKBOX" NAME="Hurl"
    VALUE="HurlBalloon"> Hurl a balloon!
<INPUT TYPE="CHECKBOX" NAME="Lob"
    VALUE="LobBalloon"> Lob a balloon!<P>
<INPUT TYPE="RADIO" NAME="Prank" VALUE="Do"
    CHECKED>Do it—it'll be funny!<BR>
<INPUT TYPE="RADIO" NAME="Prank"
    VALUE="DoNot">Don't play a prank, meanie!<BR>
<INPUT TYPE="RADIO" NAME="Prank"
    VALUE="DoNotCare">I couldn't care less. They're
    your cats, and you'll have to live with
    yourself.<P>
<INPUT SIZE=35 TYPE="TEXT" NAME="name">Your Name<P>
<SELECT SIZE=3 MULTIPLE NAME="Method">
<OPTION VALUE="single">Single Balloon
<OPTION VALUE="multiple">Multiple Balloons
<OPTION VALUE="hose">Just Use the Hose
</SELECT><P>
<INPUT TYPE="SUBMIT" VALUE="Submit">
<INPUT TYPE="RESET" VALUE="Reset">
</FORM>
```

To add a text area to your form, use the following steps:

1. Insert the `<TEXTAREA>` tags into your document and a tag
(`<P>` or `<BR>`) to force a line break after the area, as follows:

```
<TEXTAREA>
</TEXTAREA><P>
<INPUT TYPE="SUBMIT" VALUE="Submit">
<INPUT TYPE="RESET" VALUE="Reset">
</FORM>
```

2. Add the NAME attribute to the tag, as shown here:

```
<TEXTAREA NAME="comments">
</TEXTAREA><P>
```

3. Add the ROWS and COLS attributes to set the size of the area,
as in the following example:

```
<TEXTAREA NAME="comments" ROWS=3 COLS=40>
</TEXTAREA><P>
```

To include an example of suggested comments or to just tell
people that they're really supposed to enter something, you
can include the sample text between the `<TEXTAREA>` and
`</TEXTAREA>` tags. You end up with source code and output
similar to the following examples:

```
<TEXTAREA NAME="comments" ROWS=3 COLS=40>
Enter your comments here.
</TEXTAREA><P>
```

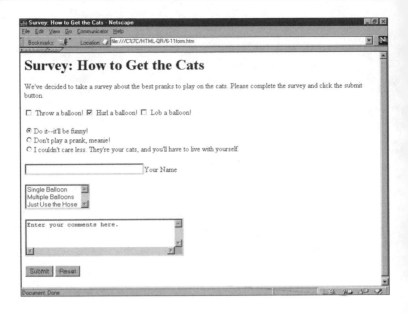

TIP

Size the text area appropriately for the information that you're trying to collect. Make the "What do you like about this page?" area, for example, much bigger than the "How do you really think we should treat our cats?" area.

Framing Your Site

In Part VII, we step into a whole new realm of HTML: *frames*. Frames let you have several different HTML documents visible within a single browser window, providing at least the possibility for visually interesting or easy-to-navigate sites. Of course, a framed site also makes you look like the HTML pro that you are.

Frames can get a little confusing at times, and the troubleshooting process isn't always the easiest. If you've gotten this far with HTML, however, nothing in here should be a real problem. Just take things one step at a time.

See also Part II for information about tags if you need a quick brush-up on using them. In this part, we don't address tag basics — we just tell you to apply them.

In this part . . .

- ✓ **Finding out about frames**
- ✓ **Creating content**
- ✓ **Making extra content for other browsers**
- ✓ **Setting up a frameset document**
- ✓ **Setting up frames**
- ✓ **Targeting frames with links**
- ✓ **Testing your framed site**

About Frames

Frames divide a browser window into several parts, just as a window (the glass kind) can be divided into several panes. Each frame (or pane) consists of an individual HTML document. In effect, using frames enables you to put multiple separate HTML documents on a single page, each in an individual box.

You can use frames to create a variety of layouts. You may, for example, have seen frames used as a navigational aid, such as a frame with links on the left side of the browser window, as shown in the following figure. After readers select a link from the left frame, the linked document appears in the right frame — thus the navigational features stay visible at all times.

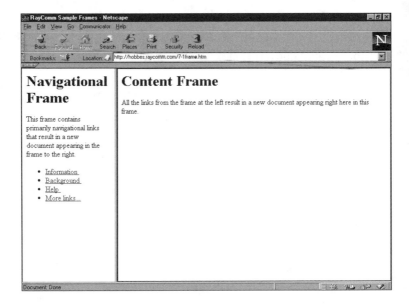

Or you may have seen frames used to help promote a corporate name or image. The logo and information, for example, appear in the top frame, and the linked documents appear in the bottom frame, as shown in the following figure.

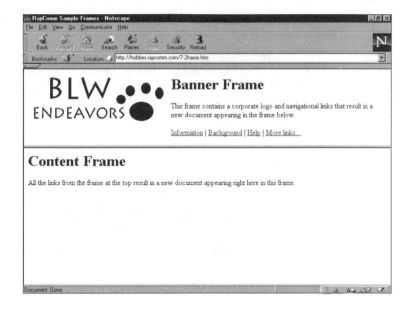

Think of these frames as being a two-column or two-row table. In these examples, the smaller of the two frames stays constant on the Web page (we call this the *navigation* or *banner document*), while the larger frame changes to display various HTML documents in the site (we call these the *content documents*). The effect is that you can develop the banner or navigation document only one time, throw it in a frame, and then be done with it — not to mention that the frame can stay visible and fixed while other text within the same overall browser window moves.

You can provide more than two frames in a browser window, but that quickly becomes very complex for both you the author and your readers. Two or (in extreme cases) three frames are plenty.

Frames do have a few disadvantages to consider: Not all browsers can display them; not all readers like them. That said, most browsers can display them; if you do them well, your readers can at least tolerate them.

Creating a framed site requires planning above all else. First, sit down and sketch out where your frames should go and give them names. (No, not names like Joey and Sam.) We'd suggest informative names such as "banner" and "body" or "index" and "text." You should also note on your sketch which frame provides the navigation or banner page (and therefore stays constant) and which frame provides the content pages (and therefore changes).

Planning this information now helps you develop content, set up the frames, and set up navigation between the frames.

For the sample site, we want the corporate logo and some navigational links in the top frame, which should take only about 20 percent (about 100 pixels) of the total area of the window. We plan to use the top frame primarily as a navigation tool, with the bottom frame the one to change with each link. Here's our sketch, complete with names:

banner

To be approx. 100 pixels high

(maybe 20% of window).

Will be used for navigation.

body

To occupy remainder of window.

Will contain content for site.

After you finish the planning and sketching, you should complete the following steps, each of which is discussed in the following sections:

1. Develop content for each frame.

2. Develop alternative content for browsers that can't accommodate frames.

3. Establish the layout or structure.

4. Set up the frames.

Developing Content

Developing content for your framed Web site doesn't really pose unique challenges, because the content is just a bunch of HTML documents, just like the ones you've done so far. In fact, if you want to add frames to an existing site, you can still use most of the existing documents with your new frames. If, on the other hand, you're creating a new site, you still must provide content at some point, and this point is as good a time as any.

Start by developing an HTML document and include content for the navigational or banner page. In the example, we start with the content for top frame, which is to contain the corporate logo and some navigational links. So far, your HTML document should look just like other HTML documents you've created.

Because frames that contain corporate logos and navigation links remain visible most of the time, you need to make sure that they look good. You can use any colors and formatting that you'd use in other HTML documents in your framed documents — what's more, you can be very sure that browsers that accommodate frames also accommodate the layout bells and whistles that you like.

Next, you should develop the content for the content pages, creating HTML documents just as you've done so far. In the process, do remember a couple of items about the remaining content pages of your framed site:

+ Don't duplicate too much information on your content pages that appears on the navigation or banner page. If, for example, your top banner — like ours — has the corporate logo, omit that item from the individual pages. And if you include a navigation page, you don't need to include navigation in your content pages.

+ Do provide some contact and identification information from your content pages. Readers could possibly access content pages directly, without going through the frames (because the pages are just HTML documents, after all), and if you have no contact or identification information, nobody knows where the pages came from.

Remember the names of your content pages — you need them as you fill in your frames.

Developing Alternative Content

Because not all browsers accommodate frames (and not all readers choose to display frames), you need to provide "alternative" content. This alternative content is similar to alternative text you include with images (you did remember to include alternative text with your images, didn't you?) that appears in place of images, in case your readers can't or choose not to view your images.

See also Part IV, specifically the section "Adding Images," for more information about alternative text.

In an ideal world, you could take the time to have two complete Web sites — one optimized for nonframed browsers and the other for framed browsers. Realistically, however, you're not likely to have the time for this luxury, because having two sites would double the time required to create and maintain these sites.

Instead, just make a single HTML document that includes all the corporate logos and links that your main frames have, and make sure that you include links to all the other pages — the ones that also appear within the frames for the lucky readers. In this alternative content document, you can be as fancy as you want, but keep in mind that browsers that can accommodate cutting edge formatting can also probably accommodate frames.

Establishing Layout Document

After you develop the content — both for the frames and alternative content, you're ready to set up your layout or *frameset document*. The frameset document tells the browser what frames are available and where they go, in addition to containing some content that only the nonframed browsers can see.

You use the tags listed in the following table to start developing a frameset document.

Tag or Attribute	Description	Use in Pairs
`<FRAMESET>` . . . `</FRAMESET>`	Establishes frame layout.	Yes
`BORDER=n`	Specifies width of border for all contained frames in pixels.	No
`BORDERCOLOR=#rrggbb` or `name`	Specifies color for contained frames.	No

Tag or Attribute	Description	Use in Pairs
COLS="n,n"	Specifies column dimensions in pixels, percentage, or in terms of remaining space (COLS="25%, 100, *").	No
FRAMEBORDER=n	Specifies border (1) or no border (0).	No
FRAMESPACING=n	Specifies space between frames, in pixels.	No
ROWS=n,n	Specifies row dimensions in pixels, percentage, or in terms of remaining space. (ROWS=25%, 100, *).	No
<NOFRAMES>. . . </NOFRAMES>	Specifies area of layout document that is visible to frame-incapable browsers.	Yes

Use the process described in the following steps to set up your frameset document:

1. Create a new HTML document that contains the <HTML>, <HEAD>, and <TITLE> tags, as shown in the following example.

In this document, do *not* use the <BODY> or !DOCTYPE tags.

```
<HTML>
<HEAD><TITLE>BLW, Inc.</TITLE></HEAD>
</HTML>
```

2. Add a <FRAMESET> tag pair, as follows:

```
<HTML>
<HEAD><TITLE>BLW, Inc.</TITLE></HEAD>
<FRAMESET>
</FRAMESET>
</HTML>
```

In more complex documents, you could have multiple tags to add frames within frames, but that's not necessary in this example.

This example sets up two rows — and no columns — so you need to add a ROWS= attribute to the <FRAMESET> tag. The first (top) row is 100 pixels high, while the remaining row fills the remaining available space, so the complete attribute is ROWS="100,*".

3. Add the ROWS= attribute, as follows:

```
<FRAMESET ROWS="100,*">
</FRAMESET>
```

We could also specify something such as `ROWS="25%,*"` to make the first row take 25 percent of the window and the second take the rest.

4. If you want to remove the frame borders (kind of a neat effect), add the `BORDER=0` and `FRAMEBORDER=0` attributes to the tag, as follows:

```
<FRAMESET ROWS="100,* BORDER=0 FRAMEBORDER=0>
</FRAMESET>
```

Why two tags? One for Netscape Navigator and one for Internet Explorer — dueling standards require special accommodations.

5. Add a `<NOFRAMES>` tag pair under the `<FRAMESET>` tag to accommodate browsers that cannot display frames, as shown here:

```
<FRAMESET ROWS="100,* BORDER=0 FRAMEBORDER=0>
</FRAMESET>
<NOFRAMES>
</NOFRAMES>
```

6. Provide regular HTML code between the `<NOFRAMES>` tags for readers with frame-incapable browsers to see, as the following example shows.

A brief identification and link to the extra content is plenty.

```
<FRAMESET ROWS="100,* BORDER=0 FRAMEBORDER=0>
</FRAMESET>
<NOFRAMES>
<H1>Welcome to BLW Enterprises!</H1>
<A HREF="noframes.html">Please join us!</A>
</NOFRAMES>
```

A tradition on the Internet is to use this space to berate readers for using older browsers. We prefer to assume that the readers are using the browser they choose to use — and which browser they choose is none of our business, so we just welcome them to the site and send them to the nonframed pages if necessary.

That takes care of establishing the actual structure of the site.

Setting Up Frames

Between the `<FRAMESET>` tags go `<FRAME>` tags to actually build the frames — one frame tag per column or row called for in the `<FRAMESET>` tag. So, for this example, we need two `<FRAME>` tags plus the associated attributes. The following table shows the tags and attributes necessary to create frames.

Tag or Attribute	Description	Use in Pairs
<FRAME>	Establishes frame.	No
BORDER=n	Specifies width of border in pixels.	No
FRAMEBORDER=n	Specifies border (1) or no border (0).	No
NAME=". . ."	Provides frame name.	No
NORESIZE	Prevents reader from resizing frame.	No
SCROLLING=". . ."	Specifies whether the frame can scroll in terms of YES, NO, or AUTO(matic). Yes requires scrollbars; No prohibits them.	No
SRC="URL"	Identifies source file that flows into frame.	No

Note: At this point, we assume that you have a complete layout document and need only to add the <FRAME> tags. The following example builds on the previous one:

```
<HTML>
<HEAD><TITLE>BLW, Inc.</TITLE></HEAD>
<FRAMESET ROWS="100,* BORDER=0 FRAMEBORDER=0>
</FRAMESET>
<NOFRAMES>
<H1>Welcome to BLW Enterprises!</H1>
<A HREF="noframes.html">Please join us!</A>
</NOFRAMES>
</HTML>
```

Follow these steps:

1. Add the first <FRAME> tag, corresponding to the top (banner) frame from the example, as follows:

```
<FRAMESET ROWS="100,* BORDER=0 FRAMEBORDER=0>
<FRAME>
</FRAMESET>
```

2. Add the SRC= attribute, which uses a standard URL (absolute or relative) to point to the document that is to fill this frame, as shown in the following example.

This document is one of the documents we developed for our content in a preceding section of this part ("Developing Content," to be precise).

```
<FRAME SRC="banner.htm">
```

3. Add the NAME= attribute to name the frame so that you can refer to it later within HTML documents, as shown here.

We're calling this one *banner* because it acts as a banner at the top of the page.

```
<FRAME SRC="banner.htm" NAME="banner">
```

4. Add other attributes, if you want — for example, those that follow.

The <FRAMESET> tag turned off the borders, but that can, optionally, also be done in each individual frame. Because the banner.htm document is primarily an image of a known size, we turn off the scrollbars and prevent readers from resizing the frame. This setup gives us a little extra layout control but could cause real problems for readers if we accidentally put more content in banner.htm than fits in the available space.

```
<FRAME SRC="banner.htm" NAME="banner" NORESIZE
  SCROLLING=NO>
```

5. Add the remaining <FRAME> tags and attributes, as follows:

```
<FRAME SRC="banner.htm" NAME="banner" NORESIZE
  SCROLLING=NO>
<FRAME SRC="main.htm" NAME="content"
  SCROLLING=AUTO>
```

We choose not to restrict either scrolling or resizing for the content frame — we anticipate that readers probably need to scroll to see all the text and don't want to cause problems. We have no concrete reason to disable those options, so we don't.

Now your frames are complete — so open up your frameset document in your browser and check out the frames. If you've been following this example, you may have frames that appear similar to those shown in the following figure.

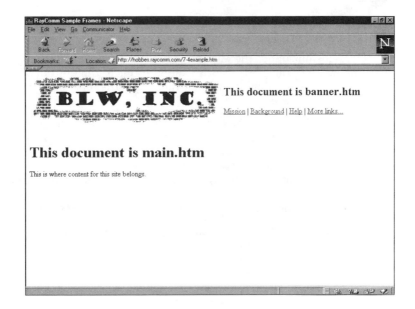

The next step is to make sure that links work correctly and bring up a page in the appropriate window.

Setting Up Links and Targets

If you've been experimenting with the frames, you may have noticed that some links appear in a completely new window, some appear in the same frame, and some appear in different frames. You, too, can control those links as well. And doing so is easy.

You use an additional attribute, as shown in the following table, for the <A> tag.

Attribute	Effect	Use in Pairs?
TARGET="..."	Specifies the default TARGET for links from framed pages.	No

Each of your links from a framed page should have the additional TARGET= attribute to name the frame in which the link should appear. The previous examples named the top frame "banner" and the lower frame "content," so links would be targeted accordingly.

To establish a link from the banner.htm document (contained in the banner frame) to the document called mission.htm (which appears within the content frame), add the following TARGET attribute to the existing link:

```
<A HREF="mission.htm" TARGET="content">Mission
   Statement</A>
```

This link opens the Mission Statement (mission.htm) in the content frame, which is the larger frame at the bottom of the browser window. If you omit the target, the link opens in the same frame as the anchor.

Additionally, you have a couple of *"magic" target names:* _top and _window being the most common and useful. If you target _top, the link replaces your frames in the same window and returns you to a nonframed environment. If you target _window, the link appears in a completely new window. This situation is handy if you're linking to another site or set of documents — your pages remain open while the others are also easily accessible.

Within a Web site, for example, you may suggest that readers access the Dummies home page at www.dummies.com. You probably wouldn't want the Dummies page to appear within one of your frames, however — that'd look silly. You need, therefore, to break out of the frames by using the _window magic target. Your framed site remains open and a new browser window appears with the Dummies home page in it. Just use code such as the following example:

```
<A HREF="http://www.dummies.com/"
   TARGET="_window">Dummies Home Page</A>
```

In addition to working in the <A> tag, the TARGET= attribute works in any other link, such as an imagemap or in a form. (The form results appear in the targeted frame.)

Testing, Testing — Again

After you completely set up your framed site, you want to extensively test the site to make sure that all the pages and links work as you'd hoped. Beyond the obvious step of opening your frameset document in a browser and clicking all the links, a few other tips may make the process a little easier:

+ If you edit the frameset document and want to make sure that you reload the changes, click the Location line with the mouse and then press Enter. If you're sure that you've made and saved layout document changes, but they don't seem to be appearing in the browser, exit out of the browser and open it up again.

+ If you edited one of the documents within a frame and want to reload just that document, click inside the frame and then click the Reload or Refresh buttons in your browser.

+ If you can, use a browser that doesn't accommodate frames to verify that the <NOFRAMES> tags in the layout document work and look as you hope.

+ Don't forget to test the pages you set up for nonframed browsers — even though you probably can't see them, someone can.

Developing Your Web Site — Putting It All Together

Throughout this book, we introduce you to a variety of HTML tags that enable you to create some really nifty effects. Essentially, we give you the tools and a few pointers about how to use the tools advantageously. In Part VIII, we provide you with the overall process for developing a Web site and provide you with some specifics about creating effective pages within your Web site.

To help show you this process, we identify several key steps, which you should complete in the order provided. We also include a few tips that help you get through the process. These steps and tips provide you with a solid planning tool for creating Web sites, but you may need to refer to other sections for specific instructions on writing the HTML code.

In this part . . .

- ✔ Identifying who your readers are
- ✔ Determining your Web site content
- ✔ Determining your Web site organization
- ✔ Determining your Web site theme
- ✔ Creating your Web pages
- ✔ Developing navigation
- ✔ Checking your Web site

Step 1: Determining Who Your Readers Are

For whom are you developing your Web site? This question is probably the first and most important one you can ask. After all, what good is the information you provide if it's not what your audience wants or needs?

Determining who your readers are helps you determine the following items:

✦ What information to provide (and not to provide).

✦ What HTML tags you should use (and should not use).

✦ What kind(s) of organization to use.

✦ What kind(s) of navigation to use.

To figure out who your readers are, you should consider the purpose for your Web site and develop a *reader profile,* which is a compilation of information about your readers, such as what kinds of information they're looking for, their knowledge about your Web site topic, and the computer equipment they have. The following two sections provide you with questions you should ask yourself to help you figure out your Web site's purpose and help you develop a reader profile.

Considering why people may visit your site

Why may people visit your site in the first place, and what kinds of information can you provide to encourage them to come back again and again? The following bulleted list should help you start thinking about your Web site's purpose:

✦ To provide information about products and services.

✦ To provide general information about you or your company (for example, just establishing a WWW presence).

✦ To request information from your audience.

✦ To provide step-by-step instructions.

✦ To allow people to contact you or your organization to request more information. (Is enabling people to fill out forms online helpful to them, or is providing simple contact information sufficient?)

✦ To let people explore related Web sites. (Is providing links to other Web sites appropriate?)

Plan on providing substantive information to your readers. You won't get very far with your Web site if you don't provide your readers with useful information (beyond how great your company is). Your readers aren't going to keep coming back to your site if they find your information boring or irrelevant to their needs. By the same token, if readers come back just to find the same information that was there last time and the time before, they probably aren't returning again.

Developing your reader profile

In developing a reader profile, you need to consider the following two things:

✦ **What information your readers are looking for.** Readers generally fall into the following four different categories, each of which wants slightly different information:

- **Manager-types:** Managers want bottom-line information — information to help them make a decision, such as the time and cost of completing a project or purchasing materials. They read mostly because they need information to make a decision.

- **Techies:** Techies like to understand how things work and can handle more technical terminology and graphics. They read because they need the information to complete a task.

- **Average Janes (or Joes):** These people like basic terminology and lots of pictures. They read because they're interested, not because they have to.

- **Experts:** Experts like new information about a subject and read because they want to know more.

Your audience may be one of the preceding types or some combination of the types. Each of the preceding types may be represented in your audience, and each requires different treatment in your Web site.

✦ **How much they already know.** The following list may help you determine what your audience does and doesn't know:

- Do they know how to browse the Web?

- Do they know how to look up specific topics or cross-reference topics on the Web?

- How much prior knowledge about the topics can you assume the audience has?

You're far better off erring on the side of providing ample background information (even though doing so is more work) than losing some of your readers because they can't understand the concepts, terminology, or information in your site without some extra explanation.

If you're considering using some of the fancier HTML effects, you should also consider what kind(s) of browser software your audience most likely is using. Are they using new software that can interpret cutting-edge HTML effects, for example, or are they using older software that requires just the basics?

Step 2: Determining Your Web Site Content

After you identify who your readers are, you need to figure out what information you want to put in your Web site. Start by developing an outline that contains the following information:

✦ Introductory information to include on your home page.

✦ Several main topics you want to include in the Web site.

✦ Several subtopics that you want to discuss or expand.

In determining what to include in your Web site, you should have a combination of *static information* and *dynamic information*, as follows:

✦ *Static information* includes general data that doesn't often change, such as an address, contact information, and copyright information.

✦ *Dynamic information* includes variable material that you probably want to update often. You should update or modify the Web site contents frequently so that readers want to revisit your site to get fresh information.

The following figure shows examples of static and dynamic information.

Static information

Dynamic information

Static information

Step 3: Determining Your Web Site Organization

Organizing HTML documents looks pretty easy, right? Actually, developing good HTML documents takes some planning. Just letting your pages and links multiply rarely leads to clear organization. Consider the following three methods of organization (explained more thoroughly in the following sections):

✦ **Hierarchical organization:** Use this method if your documents have multiple major topics.

✦ **Linear organization:** Use this method if you present instructions or a process.

✦ **Webbed organization:** Use this method if you want readers to cross-reference information on other pages.

Choosing and applying these organizational methods, sometimes used in combination, makes finding the information you're providing much easier for your readers. A great way to figure out which type of organization you should use is to sketch out on a piece of paper how you want your HTML documents linked together. Just write down all the topics and subtopics you want to include (look at the outline you developed in Step 2) and draw lines (which represent links) from topic to topic. You'll find that most of these links work in both directions — that is, a link goes from the first page to the second page and then from the second page back to the first page.

The following three sections describe the different types of organizations.

Hierarchical organization

You may choose *hierarchical organization* if you have multiple major topics. If you put your autobiography online, for example, you may want to organize it hierarchically with a main page (analogous to the table of contents and title page), chapter introduction pages, and individual sections following the chapter introduction pages. Schematically, hierarchical structure looks like the following drawing:

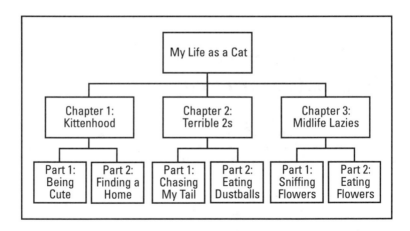

Hierarchical organization offers your readers the chance to go directly to the chapter or section of their choice. Readers interested in your exploits when you were in your 20s shouldn't need to wade through the stories of your terrible 2s to get there.

If you have more than ten documents in a hierarchical structure, you may consider creating new directories or folders for each of the major sections. Creating new directories makes maintaining the sections easier for you and helps your readers see how the whole set of documents fits together.

See also Part III for more information about URLs and linking to documents in other directories or folders.

Linear organization

You may choose *linear organization* if you put instructions online. If you're describing the instructions to a nuclear power plant, for example, you want the reader to go through all of the safety instructions before reading anything else. Allowing the reader to jump directly to the "fire it up" section is not in anyone's best interest. Linear structure looks like the following drawing.

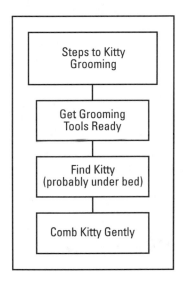

Linear organization can frustrate readers if they find themselves moving from page to page without a link to take them back to your home page or at least a link to break out of the sequence of pages. Don't deprive your readers of an escape — unless you *are* documenting instructions for a nuclear power plant.

Webbed organization

You may also choose *webbed organization,* in which pages link to many other pages. Documents with lots of cross-references will look like this:

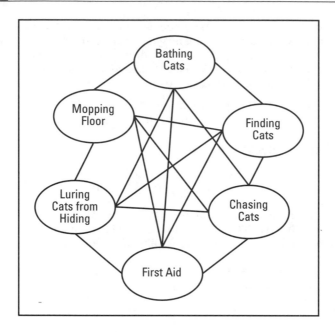

Although webbed organization looks really cool, keep in mind that readers can easily get "lost in hyperspace." If you choose this method, make sure that you include a link on each page to let readers go back to a home page to get their bearings.

As you construct your menus and links, don't put too many levels of menus between your readers and the information. If readers must plow through three or four menu levels between your home page and the information they're looking for, they're likely to give up.

Step 4: Establishing a Web Site Theme

Every Web site should have a theme that helps unify pages into an entire site. You can create a theme for your Web site by performing one or more of the following tasks:

✦ **Using a background.** You can use one background color, pattern, or image throughout your Web site.

✦ **Using a color scheme.** You can use consistent colors for text, links, visited links, or active links.

✦ **Using a logo.** You can create a logo for your Web site that shows up on every page.

♦ **Using a repeating graphic** — a small one. You can use a small graphic (such as a logo graphic) that appears on every page.

♦ **Using a header or footer.** You can use headers or footers that provide constant information from page to page.

See also Part VI for more information about automatically including stuff on pages.

Step 5: Generating Your Web Site

Here you go! You're ready to create your Web site by using the information you determined in Steps 1 through 4. Creating the site is, relative to the other steps, the easy part of the process. While establishing your Web site, you need to pay close attention to creating the home page, using conventions that help make reading easier, and polishing your work.

Creating an effective home page

A *home page* is simply a common term for the starting point of a set of HTML documents on the Internet. The home page is where you typically introduce a topic and provide links to other information about that topic. Your home page should be the starting point for all those topics you outlined in Steps 2 and 3.

Your home page should include the following essential items:

♦ **Last revision date:** Shows the date that you last revised your home page, which indicates to a user how current the information is.

♦ **Contact and author information:** Allows a user to follow up on anything they see (or don't see) in your documents.

See also Part V for nifty ways to provide contact information.

Home page content should generally include at least the following information:

♦ If your home page is a stand-alone page — that is, it's not just a menu of links pointing to other (content-filled) pages — you obviously want to include all your information on the one page.

♦ If your home page is mainly a pointer to pages (for example, a menu of useful pointers you've found on the Internet), you should include introductory-type information (such as a brief overview or summary) on your home page, along with a navigation tool.

✦ If your home page links your other pages together, your home page also needs to include a navigation tool that not only provides direct links to other pages but also shows a user what other information is available.

The information that you provide in your home pages can vary greatly. Your pages don't need to look like anyone else's pages, and you're free to shuffle the content around as often as you please. The idea is to provide enough information so that readers get the gist of the content without wasting time with fluff or clutter.

Your home page is a great place to make announcements or to provide high-priority information. Keep in mind that your home page may be the only page that a user visits!

Making readers happy

You also need to consider how to help keep readers glued to your Web site. Readers generally browse through Web sites one of two ways:

✦ They *skim* (looking for specific information).

✦ They *scan* (browsing to see what information is available).

To help readers skim and scan online documents, follow these guidelines:

✦ **Make your Web pages snazzy.** You can include fancy effects such as graphics, imagemaps, frames, tables, and forms to make your site more interesting. Don't go overboard, however! Remember that some of these fancier effects take longer to download and, therefore, make your readers wait and wait.

✦ **Use informative headings and subheadings to announce topics.** Every time you change topics, you should include a new heading or subheading that describes or summarizes the new content. Thumb through this book, for example, and see how the headings and subheadings help you easily spot information.

The following two figures show how headings help improve skimming and scanning — the first is before and second after adding headings.

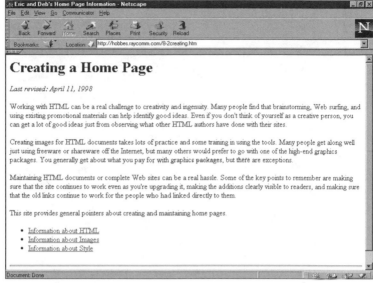

✦ **Use bulleted and numbered lists to provide "at-a-glance" information.** Consider the following figure, which shows the same information (same text) organized in two different ways. We bet that you find the bulleted information easier to read, too.

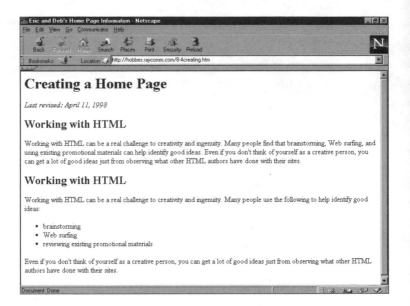

Here are some useful guidelines to follow in creating lists:

✦ **Start each list item with the same part of speech.** That is, start each list item with a noun, a verb, an adjective, or a gerund (those verbs with *-ing* endings). In most cases, the part of speech you use to start your list items doesn't really matter as long as you're consistent within the list. See the list in the preceding figure for an example.

✦ **Don't make lists too long.** Lists that are longer than seven items can sometimes be as difficult to read as long paragraphs.

✦ **Put the most important information first.** If you have more than one main point, break the points into separate items.

✦ *Chunk,* **or group, similar information together.** By chunking, you help readers locate all the information about a given topic without their needing to search the entire document.

Polishing your work

A very easy, but often overlooked, task in completing your HTML documents is to proofread and edit your pages carefully. Carelessness here can undo all your hard work.

We know that spell-checking and proofreading sound like simple suggestions — of course you're going to proofread your documents. If you take a quick look around at many of the pages on the Internet, however, you find that these little picky grammar problems abound. If you're concerned with your image, make sure that you pay careful attention to details such as spelling and proofreading.

Ensuring that your documents are free from these errors is essential for several reasons:

✦ Numerous spelling and proofreading errors can detract from the content and cause confusion or frustration for your readers.

✦ Numerous errors slow down reading speed for your readers.

✦ Poor writing can irritate readers to the extent that they don't read past your home page or ever visit your Web site again.

✦ The overall document quality helps determine how well your readers understand the content.

To help eliminate spelling and proofreading errors, follow these guidelines:

✦ Use a spell-checker if one is available in the text editor. (Careful here — spell-checkers *don't* catch everything!)

✦ Ask someone else to read your documents.

✦ Read the documents out loud. (This technique is especially helpful for finding proofreading errors.)

✦ Check for editing or proofreading errors in both the text editor and the browser.

Step 6: Producing Navigation Tools

Back in Step 3 of this process, you determined the organization of the Web site and determined which pages link. Now you need to develop the *navigation tools* that your readers use to leap from page to page. You can use any of the following as links:

✦ Key words that you link to related documents.

✦ Buttons, or *icons,* that direct readers to related documents.

✦ Entire images that link readers to related information.

See also Part III for more information about links and Part IV for information about using images to link to other documents.

Placing navigation tools

One of the most important aspects of creating navigation tools is where you place them on the page. You can place navigation tools at the top, middle, or bottom of your HTML document, or you can use a combination of these arrangements.

Consider the needs of your users as you place the navigation tools — consider the location that's the easiest one for them to use. In general, follow these guidelines:

✦ **Provide more than one navigation method.** A good idea is to provide more than one way for readers to navigate through the document (for example, text links, buttons and an imagemap).

✦ **Provide more than one navigation location.** Include navigation options at both the top and bottom of each page, or, if appropriate, put the navigational information in an adjacent frame. This way, readers don't need to scroll up and down pages so much to find links to new information.

✦ **Use consistent navigation devices throughout the document.** As you're developing a series of HTML documents, choose the methods of navigation you want — and stick to them. If you want navigation buttons and text links to appear at the top of a page, include those devices in the same place on every page.

Using top and bottom navigation effectively

The most common place to put navigation tools is at the top or the bottom of the page. Each option offers several advantages and disadvantages.

A top-navigation tool performs the following functions:

✦ Allows readers to see navigation choices immediately. (But it also requires readers to scroll back to the top to use the navigation tool.)

✦ Lets readers skip a page easily (for example, if they arrive at a page in error).

A bottom-navigation tool performs the following functions:

✦ Enables readers to access navigation choices after they finish the page without needing to scroll back to the top.

✦ Requires readers to go through the entire page to get to the navigation choices. (This requirement can be good or bad. It forces readers to go through pages, but you need to keep in mind that they may get tired of doing so and give up on your Web site completely.)

Remember to consider what your users want and need. You can, for example, provide a complete navigation list at the top of your page and provide links to the previous and next pages at the bottom. Or you can even put navigation tools in the middle of HTML pages if the pages are particularly long. Just try to imagine what your readers would find most useful — and do it!

Creating navigation tools

Creating navigation tools is easy. Just determine what kind of links to include and provide the links in places that users can easily access. The links that you include can be links to other parts of the same document or links to related documents.

To include navigation tools in your HTML documents, follow these steps:

1. Determine what types of links you want to include.

2. Determine where you want to place the navigation tool(s) on your Web page (for example, at the top, in the middle, or at the bottom of the Web page).

3. Insert the navigation tools in the HTML pages.

Your navigation tools are a series of links to the previous and following pages in the sequence the pages should be read.

4. Check the navigation by opening the document in your browser.

Go through each page and try each navigation choice.

Not every page needs to include a comprehensive list of navigation choices (as the home page may), but each page should include navigation choices to the following:

✦ The previous page in sequence, if applicable.

✦ The next page in sequence, if applicable.

✦ The home page.

The following example shows you how to create the navigational links (or menu) for documents in an alphabetic sequence. We walk you through the a.html, b.html, and c.html documents. You're on your own for d.html through z.html. Follow this example to generate links to the previous document, back to the home page, and to the next document. Obviously, the process applies to any linear sequence of documents.

Note: Before beginning these steps, make sure that you open your browser and text editor. You can apply these steps to a new document or you can apply this information to an existing document.

Follow these steps:

1. Open the first document in sequence (a.html, in this case).

2. Type the text that you want to use for the links at the bottom of the file — for example, that shown in the following example:

```
Previous | Home Page | Next
```

3. Add a link to the home page, as shown in the following example.

Because you started in the a.html document, no previous document exists in this sequence. The first link you add, therefore, is to the home page text.

```
Previous | <A HREF="homepage.html">Home Page
</A> | Next
```

4. Add a link from Next to the b.html document, as follows:

```
Previous | <A HREF="homepage.html">Home Page
</A> | <A HREF="b.html">Next</A>
```

5. Save and close a.html and open b.html to enter the next set of links.

6. Type the text that you want to use for the links at the bottom of the file, as shown here:

```
Previous | Home Page | Next
```

7. Add a link from Previous back to a.html, as follows:

```
<A HREF="a.html">Previous</A> | Home Page |
Next
```

8. Add a link from Home Page back to the home page, as shown in this example:

```
<A HREF="a.html">Previous</A> |
<A HREF="homepage.html">Home Page</A> | Next
```

If you think that copying and pasting the links from one document to another can speed things up, you're right. You don't need to add the link to the home page and you just edit the rest of the links. Copying and pasting, however, really increases your chances of having messed up links. Be careful!

9. Add a link from Next to c.html, as follows:

```
<A HREF="a.html">Previous</A> |
<A HREF="homepage.html">Home Page</A> |
<A HREF="c.html">Next</A>
```

10. Save and close b.html and open c.html to enter the next set of links.

11. Type the text you want to use for the links at the bottom of the file, as shown here:

```
Previous | Home Page | Next
```

12. Add a link from Previous back to b.html, as follows:

```
<A HREF="b.html">Previous</A> | Home Page |
    Next
```

13. Add a link from Home Page back to the home page, as the following example shows:

```
<A HREF="b.html">Previous</A> |
<A HREF="homepage.html">Home Page</A> | Next
```

14. Add a link from Next to d.html, as follows:

```
<A HREF="b.html">Previous</A> |
<A HREF="homepage.html">Home Page</A> |
<A HREF="d.html">Next</A>
```

Make sure that you test your links thoroughly! As repetitive as creating the links is, it's easy to get careless.

Creating navigational tools is easier if you use the same terminology on each type of choice. Words such as *next* and *previous* are good choices. Customized links such as *Back to A* and *Forward to C,* however, are easier for your readers to use.

Additionally, you could use icons with arrows or letters on them within the link to make your page a little more visually interesting.

Step 7: Testing Your Web Site

Testing your Web site is one of the most important steps in this process. Testing just means to check the site for problems, such as the following:

+ Incorrect navigation (navigation that doesn't work or links to the wrong information).

+ Spelling and proofreading errors.

+ Missing or incorrect graphics.

+ Alignment problems with text and graphics.

+ Alignment problems with list items.

+ Incomplete closing tags. (For example, if you forget to close a <B> tag, the bold typeface runs on and on.)

If you can, try to view your Web page through more than one Web browser. If you've been looking at your work by using only Netscape, for example, you may want to take a look at it in Internet Explorer. *See also* Part I for samples of a Web page seen in different Web browsers.

Validation services are essentially computer programs that test your pages to see whether the HTML code is standard and that you haven't made any technical mistakes. Validation services aren't perfect, any more than spell-checkers or grammar-checkers are, but they do give an additional check to your documents to help make sure that you haven't forgotten some closing tags or made other technical errors.

Validation services are available on the Internet either as specialized Web sites or as programs you can download. If you choose to download the software, you can check your site before it ever sees the light of day. On the other hand, using an online validation service is probably somewhat easier than the software version — you just submit your URL and wait for the results.

We recommend Web Techs Validation Service at http://www.webtechs.com/html-val-svc/ and really do recommend taking this last step to ensure that you have a great Web site.

HTML Tags

Appendix A provides you with a comprehensive list of HTML tags and attributes. Much of the information provided in these tables is discussed in detail in this book; some of the tags and attributes, however, are provided for you to reference as your HTML skills improve and expand.

The tables in Appendix A cover the following:

+ **HTML Structural Markup** — includes HTML structure tags, document characteristics, tags, and attributes.

+ **HTML Body Markup** — includes sectional formatting tags that fall within the body.

+ **List Markup** — includes tags and attributes for creating lists.

+ **Character-level Markup** — includes HTML tags and attributes used to specify character-level formatting.

+ **Hypertext Anchors and Links Markup** — includes tags and attributes used to create links and anchors.

+ **Image Markup** — includes tags and attributes for including images in HTML documents.

+ **Table and Column Markup** — includes tags and attributes for creating tables.

+ **Form Markup** — includes tags and attributes for using forms within a document.

+ **Frames and Layers Markup** — includes tags and attributes for developing frames and layers.

+ **Script Markup** — includes tags and attributes for using scripts in HTML documents.

+ **Style Sheet Markup** — includes tags and attributes for using style sheets in HTML documents.

+ **Internet Explorer Multimedia Extensions** — includes tags and attributes for adding multimedia to HTML documents. These work with only Microsoft's Internet Explorer (as of press time).

+ **Embedded Applets and Objects** — includes tag and attributes to include programs or objects within an HTML document.

The tables in this appendix are divided into three columns:

+ The *Markup* column provides the specific HTML tag or attribute. Tags are enclosed in pointed brackets; attributes follow the associated tag and in italics. The markup is generally alphabetized by tags, but closely related tags do appear together, regardless of their place in the alphabet. Additionally, tags that are particularly esoteric or not widely accepted are located at the end of the tables.

Additionally, many attributes appear under several different tags. Rather than extensively cross-referencing the attributes, we include them in every place that they apply — the easier to look up the attributes, the better!

✦ The *Description* column provides a description of each tag and attribute and minimal guidance about use. In general, characteristics in ALL CAPS are exactly what you may fill in for the "..." in the tables. Please refer to the body of the book for specific instructions. Tags that are not extensively discussed in the book are likely to be fairly similar to other tags — feel free to experiment.

A ✓ in this column indicates that, at time of publication, approximately 75 percent or more of the browsers in use support the tag. Generally speaking, that means that the most common versions of both Internet Explorer and Netscape Navigator support the tag. Using checked tags, however, could still exclude up to 25 percent of your potential audience.

Tags labeled as HTML 3.2, CSSI, Script, or Frames in the *Reference or Usage* column are likely to gain acceptance over time.

Tags and attributes included in Netscape and Internet Explorer (labeled Navigator/IE, or IE/Navigator, depending on the better support) work only if the reader is using those specific browser packages. If a tag is available only in Navigator or Internet Explorer, be advised that it may never gain wider acceptance.

Table A-1   *Structural Markup*

Markup	Description	Reference or Usage
`<!DOCTYPE HTML PUBLIC "-// W3C//DTD HTML 3.2 Final//EN">`	✓ Identifies document as conforming to the HTML specification. Required at top of all HTML documents. Mandatory in HTML 3.2.	HTML 2.0
`<HTML>. . . </HTML>`	✓ Encloses the entire document and identifies it as HTML.	HTML 2.0
`<HEAD>. . . </HEAD>`	✓ Sets off the document header information, including the title.	HTML 2.0
`<TITLE>. . . </TITLE>`	✓ Encloses the document title. Mandatory in HTML 3.2.	HTML 2.0
`<BASE>`	✓ Specifies general document link information about the current file so that links and relative URLs are interpreted correctly. Use only if necessary in your specific application.	HTML 2.0

(continued)

Table A-1 (continued)

Markup	Description	Reference or Usage
HREF="URL"	✓ Specifies the URL of current file so that relative URLs are interpreted correctly.	HTML 2.0
TARGET=". . ."	✓ Specifies the default target for links from framed pages.	Frames
<LINK>	Specifies the general relationships of the current document to other documents. Recognized by very few browsers.	HTML 2.0
REV=MADE HREF= "http:// url.com"	Identifies author or URL. Other link attributes exist but are seldom used or recognized by browsers.	HTML 2.0
REL=STYLESHEET TYPE="text/css" HREF="URL"	Links CSS1 Stylesheet.	CSSI
<META . . . >	✓ Provides information about the document attributes. Could include CONTENT, NAME= and HTTP-EQUIV=).	HTML 2.0
NAME=". . ."	✓ Identifies a type of header or indexing information for the document (e.g., KEYWORDS, DESCRIPTION).	HTML 2.0
CONTENT=". . ."	✓ Provides information about the document, based on other attribute in the same <META> tag.	HTML 2.0
HTTP-EQUIV=	Can replace NAME= attribute and causes special document header information to be sent by a Web server.	HTML 2.0
CHARSET=	Identifies the document's character set for use by non-English languages.	IE
<BODY>. . . </BODY>	✓ Identifies all information included in the main portion (body) of the document.	HTML 2.0
ALINK="#rrggbb" or "name"	✓ Colors the links in your document based on the rrggbb number or the standard color name. ALINK stands for the active link.	HTML 3.2
BACKGROUND="URL"	✓ Places an image behind the text in your HTML document.	HTML 3.2
BGCOLOR= "#rrggbb" or "name"	✓ Colors the background based on the rrggbb number or the standard color name.	HTML 3.2
BGPROPERTIES= fixed	Specifies a nonscrolling background image.	IE

Markup	Description	Reference or Usage
LEFTMARGIN=n	Specifies the left margin for the entire body of the page in pixels.	IE
LINK="#rrggbb" or *"name"*	✓ Colors the links in your document based on the rrggbb number or the standard color name. LINK is for the anchor text visible in the document.	HTML 3.2
TEXT="#rrggbb" or *"name"*	✓ Colors all the normal text in the document based on the rrggbb number or the standard color name.	HTML 3.2
TOPMARGIN=n	Specifies the margin for the top of the page in pixels.	IE
VLINK="#rrggbb" or *"name"*	✓ Colors the visited links in your document based on the rrggbb number or the standard color name. VLINK stands for visited link.	HTML 3.2

Table A-2   **Body Markup**

Markup	Description	Reference or Usage
`<!--...-->`	✓ Provides a place to insert comments. Comments are ignored by the browser yet visible in the source.	HTML 2.0
`<ADDRESS>...</ADDRESS>`	✓ Encloses information about the author and the document.	HTML 2.0
`<BLOCKQUOTE>...</BLOCKQUOTE>`	✓ Encloses a quotation.	HTML 2.0
` `	✓ Forces a line break.	HTML 2.0
CLEAR="..."	✓ Forces clear margins (below images or objects) on the LEFT, RIGHT, or BOTH.	HTML 3.2
`<DIV>...</DIV>`	Indicates a division or section within a document.	HTML 2.0
ALIGN="..."	Aligns the division (or section) to the LEFT, RIGHT, or CENTER. The tags `<CENTER>...</CENTER>` are nonstandard abbreviations of `<DIV ALIGN=CENTER>...</DIV>`.	HTML 3.2
NOWRAP	✓ Prevents text wrap within the section.	IE
LANG="..."	Indicates ISO languages used in section.	IE

(continued)

Table A-2 (continued)

Markup	Description	Reference or Usage

`<H1>. . .</H1>`
`<H2>. . .</H2>`
`<H3>. . .</H3>`
`<H4>. . .</H4>`
`<H5>. . .</H5>`
`<H6>. . .</H6>`
	✓ Indicate headings ranging from `<H1>` to `<H6>` (the least important). The `<H1>` tags are normally used for the document title or main heading.	HTML 2.0

`ALIGN=". . ."`	✓ Aligns the heading to the `LEFT`, `RIGHT`, or `CENTER`.	HTML 3.2
`NOBR`	Prevents text breaks or line wraps within tag.	Navigator
`<HR>`	✓ Specifies a horizontal rule.	HTML 3.2
`COLOR="#rrggbb"` or `"name"`	Specifies background color based on `rrggbb` or the standard color name.	IE
`SIZE=n`	✓ Indicates the width (in pixels or %) of the horizontal rule.	HTML 3.2
`WIDTH="n"`	✓ Specifies an exact width of the horizontal rule in pixels or a relative width measured as a percentage of document width.	HTML 3.2
`ALIGN=". . ."`	✓ Specifies whether the horizontal rule should be at the `LEFT`, `RIGHT`, or `CENTER`.	HTML 3.2
`NOSHADE`	✓ Prohibits horizontal rule shading.	HTML 3.2
`<NOBR>. . .` `</NOBR>`	✓ Specifies a string of elements without line breaks.	IE/ Navigator
`<P>. . .</P>`	✓ Indicates the beginning of a paragraph (the closing `</P>` tag is optional).	HTML 2.0
`ALIGN=". . ."`	✓ Aligns the paragraph to the `LEFT`, `RIGHT`, or `CENTER`.	HTML 3.2
`<PRE>. . .</PRE>`	✓ Encloses blocks of text to be shown verbatim in a fixed-width font (white space and line breaks are significant).	HTML 2.0
`WIDTH=n`	Specifies a width for the section in characters.	HTML 3.2
`<WBR>`	✓ Identifies where a line break can be inserted by the browser, if necessary, within a `<NOBR>` section.	IE/ Navigator

Table A-3   *List Markup*

Markup	Description	Reference or Usage
`<DIR>. . .</DIR>`	✓ Provides a directory list.	HTML 2.0
COMPACT	✓ Formats list to take as little space as possible.	HTML 2.0
`<DL>. . .</DL>`	✓ Provides a definition list.	HTML 2.0
`<DT>`	✓ Begins each item title in the definition list.	HTML 2.0
`<DD>`	✓ Begins each item definition in the definition list.	HTML 2.0
`<LI>`	✓ Identifies each item in a `<DIR>`, `<MENU>`, `<OL>`, or `<UL>` list.	HTML 2.0
TYPE=A, a, I, i, or 1	✓ Specifies the style of an ordered list. A = large letters; a = small letters; I = large Roman numerals; i = small Roman numerals; 1 = numbers.	HTML 3.2
VALUE=n	✓ Changes the count of ordered lists as they progress.	HTML 3.2
`<MENU>. . . </MENU>`	✓ Provides a menu list.	HTML 2.0
COMPACT	✓ Formats list to take as little space as possible.	HTML 2.0
`<OL>. . .</OL>`	✓ Specifies ordered (numbered) lists.	HTML 2.0
START=n	✓ Specifies a starting number for the list.	HTML 3.2
COMPACT	✓ Formats list to take as little space as possible.	HTML 2.0
TYPE=A, a, I, i, or 1	✓ Specifies the style of an ordered list. A=large letters; a=small letters; I = large Roman numerals; i = small Roman numerals; 1 = numbers.	HTML 3.2
`<UL>. . .</UL>`	✓ Encloses unordered lists.	HTML 2.0
COMPACT	✓ Formats list to take as little space as possible.	HTML 2.0

Table A-4   *Character-level Markup*

Markup	Description	Reference or Usage
`<B>. . .</B>`	✓ Makes text bold.	HTML 2.0
`<BASEFONT>`	✓ Specifies standard font information for the document.	HTML 3.2
`COLOR="#rrggbb"` or `"name"`	✓ Colors the text based on the `rrggbb` number or the standard color name.	IE/ Navigator
`SIZE=n`	✓ Changes the size n, on a scale from 1 to 7, of the base font, which also changes the size of fonts that are based on the base font.	HTML 3.2
`FACE=". . ."`	✓ Sets the typeface name. A list of font names can be specified.	IE/ Navigator
`<BIG>. . .</BIG>`	✓ Makes text big.	HTML 3.2
`<BLINK>. . .</BLINK>`	Makes text blink.	Navigator
`<CITE>. . .</CITE>`	✓ Marks a citation of a book, article, movie, and so on and is often displayed in italics.	HTML 2.0
`<CODE>. . .</CODE>`	✓ Marks a piece of computer source code and is often displayed in a fixed-width font.	HTML 2.0
`<DFN>. . .</DFN>`	Marks defining (first) occurrence of term.	HTML 3.2
`<EM>. . .</EM>`	✓ Emphasizes text, usually HTML, by displaying it as italics.	HTML 2.0
`<FONT>. . .</FONT>`	✓ Changes the font.	HTML 3.2
`COLOR="#rrggbb"` or `"name"`	✓ Colors the text based on the `rrggbb` number or the standard color name.	HTML 3.2
`FACE=". . ."`	✓ Sets the typeface name. A list of font names can be specified.	IE/ Navigator
`SIZE="n"`	✓ Changes the font size on a scale from 1 to 7.	HTML 3.2
`<I>. . .</I>`	✓ Makes text italic.	HTML 2.0
`<KBD>. . .</KBD>`	✓ Shows an example of a keyboard entry or user input.	HTML 2.0
`<S>. . .</S>` or `<STRIKE>. . .</STRIKE>`	✓ Overstrikes text.	HTML 2.0
`<SAMP>. . .</SAMP>`	✓ Shows literal characters, such as computer output.	HTML 2.0

Markup	Description	Reference or Usage
`<SMALL>. . .` `</SMALL>`	✓ Makes text small.	HTML 3.2
`<STRONG>. . .` `</STRONG>`	✓ Gives strong emphasis to text. Often displayed as bold.	HTML 2.0
`<SUB>. . .</SUB>`	✓ Makes text subscript.	HTML 2.0
`<SUP>. . .</SUP>`	✓ Makes text superscript.	HTML 2.0
`<TT>. . .</TT>`	✓ Creates typewriter (fixed-width) font.	HTML 2.0
`<U>. . .</U>`	✓ Underlines text.	HTML 2.0
`<VAR>. . .</VAR>`	✓ Shows the name of a variable. Often displayed as italic.	HTML 2.0
`<SPACER>`	Puts a space in your document.	Navigator
`TYPE=". . ."`	Specifies the type of space as `HORIZONTAL`, `VERTICAL`, or `BLOCK`.	Navigator
`HEIGHT=n`	Specifies height in pixels.	Navigator
`WIDTH=n`	Specifies width in pixels.	Navigator
`ALIGN=". . ."`	Specifies alignment in terms of `TOP`, `TEXTTOP`, `MIDDLE`, `ABSMIDDLE`, `BOTTOM`, `BASELINE`, `ABSBOTTOM`.	Navigator

Table A-5   *Hypertext Anchors/Links Markup*

Markup	Description	Reference or Usage
`<A>. . .</A>`	✓ Marks an anchor.	HTML 2.0
`HREF="URL"`	✓ Creates a link to the specified URL.	HTML 2.0
`TARGET=". . ."`	✓ Specifies the default `TARGET` for links from framed pages.	Frames
`TITLE=". . ."`	Identifies title or label for anchor.	HTML 3.2
`onClick=". . ."`	✓ Specifies JavaScript action to occur if `HREF` anchor is selected.	JavaScript
`onMouseOver=` `". . ."`	✓ Specifies JavaScript action to occur if mouse passes over `HREF` anchor.	JavaScript
`NAME=". . ."`	✓ Creates a named anchor.	HTML 2.0

Table A-6   *Image Markup*

Markup	Description	Reference or Usage
`<IMG>`	✓ Inserts an image.	HTML 2.0
`SRC="URL"`	✓ Specified URL of image to include.	HTML 2.0
`ALIGN="..."`	✓ Places the object within the page. RIGHT and LEFT float the object as specified and wrap text around it. MIDDLE, TOP, and BOTTOM align relative to surrounding text.	HTML 3.2
`ALT="..."`	✓ Specifies the text that should appear if the image does not.	HTML 2.0
`BORDER=n`	✓ Controls the thickness of the border around an image in pixels.	HTML 3.2
`CONTROLS`	Displays a set of video controls under the clip.	IE
`DYNSRC="URL"`	Specifies the address of a video clip or VRML world to appear in the window.	IE
`HEIGHT=n`	✓ Specifies the height of the image in pixels.	HTML 3.2
`HSPACE=n`	✓ Controls the horizontal space (white space) around the image in pixels.	HTML 3.2
`ISMAP`	✓ Specifies that the image is a server-side clickable imagemap.	HTML 2.0
`LOOP="..."`	Specifies how many times (number or "INFINITE") a video clip loops.	IE
`LOWSRC="URL"`	Specifies a low resolution image that will load first, and then be replaced by the SRC image.	Navigator
`START="..."`	Specifies when a video clip should start playing, either at FILEOPEN or at MOUSEOVER.	IE
`USEMAP="mapname"`	✓ Identifies the picture as a client-side imagemap and specifies a MAP to use for acting on the user's clicks.	HTML 3.2
`VSPACE=n`	✓ Controls the vertical space (white space) around the image in pixels.	HTML 3.2
`WIDTH=n`	✓ Specifies the width of the image in pixels.	HTML 3.2
`TITLE="..."`	Specifies title to appear with image.	IE
`<MAP>`	✓ Specifies a collection of hot spots for a client-side imagemap.	HTML 3.2

Markup	Description	Reference or Usage
NAME="..."	✓ Gives the MAP a name so it can be referred to later.	HTML 3.2
`<AREA>`	✓ Specifies the shape of a "hot spot" in a client-side imagemap.	HTML 3.2
COORDS="x1, y1, x2, y2, ..."	✓ Specifies coordinates that define the hot spot's shape.	HTML 3.2
HREF="URL"	✓ Specifies the destination of the hot spot. See above.	HTML 3.2
NOHREF	✓ Indicates that clicks in this region should cause no action.	HTML 3.2
ALT="..."	✓ Specifies the text that should be displayed if the image is not.	HTML 3.0
TARGET="..."	✓ Specifies the default TARGET for links from framed pages.	Frames
TITLE="..."	Specifies extra information to appear with image in Internet Explorer.	IE
TABINDEX=n	Specifies sequence number for readers who use the tab key to maneuver around the page.	IE
SHAPE="..."	✓ Specifies type of shape as RECT (rectangle), CIRCLE, or POLYGON.	HTML 3.2

Table A-7	*Table and Column Markup*	

Markup	Description	Reference or Usage
`<TABLE>...` `</TABLE>`	✓ Creates a table.	HTML 3.2
ALIGN="..."	✓ Aligns the table to the LEFT, RIGHT, or CENTER.	HTML 3.2
BACKGROUND="URL"	Specifies background image for the table.	IE
BORDER=n	✓ Draws borders around table cells. The number determines the size in pixels.	HTML 3.2
BGCOLOR= "#rrggbb" or "name"	Sets background color by rrggbb number or standard color name.	Navigator/IE
BORDERCOLOR= "#rrggbb" or "name"	Specifies border color by rrggbb number or standard color name and must be used with the BORDER attribute.	IE

(continued)

Table A-7 (continued)

Markup	Description	Reference or Usage
BORDERCOLORDARK= "#rrggbb" or *"name"*	Sets independent border color control by rrggbb number or standard color name for one of the two colors used to draw a 3-D border. Must be used with the BORDER attribute.	IE
BORDERCOLOR- LIGHT="#rrggbb" or *"name"*	Sets independent border color control by rrggbb number or standard color name for one of the two colors used to draw a 3-D border. Must be used with the BORDER attribute.	IE
CELLPADDING=n	✓ Inserts space between the cell border and the cell contents. The number determines the size in pixels.	HTML 3.2
CELLSPACING=n	✓ Inserts specified space between cells. The number determines the size in pixels.	HTML 3.2
CLEAR=". . ."	Specifies where text following table begins as NO (text follows table immediately), LEFT (starts as left-aligned line), RIGHT (right-aligned line), ALL (first blank line after table).	IE
FRAME=". . ."	Specifies outer border for the table as BORDER, VOID, ABOVE, BELOW, HSIDES (horizontal sides), LHS (left hand side), RHS (right hand side), VSIDES (vertical sides), BOX.	IE
RULES=". . ."	Specifies inner borders for table as GROUPS (based on IE specific table tags COLGROUP, THEAD, TBODY, TFOOT), ROWS, COLS, or ALL.	IE
COLS=n	Sets the number of columns in table.	IE
NOWRAP	Keeps table rows from wrapping if they go past the right margin.	IE
WIDTH=n	✓ Describes the table width in terms of the number of pixels or the percentage of the document width.	HTML 3.2
<CAPTION>. . . </CAPTION>	✓ Identifies table caption.	HTML 3.2
ALIGN=". . ."	✓ Aligns the text to the TOP or BOTTOM of the table.	HTML 3.2
<TR>. . .</TR>	✓ Inserts table rows.	HTML 3.2
NOWRAP	Keeps table rows from wrapping when they go past the right margin.	IE

Markup	Description	Reference or Usage
ALIGN="..."	✓ Aligns the text to the LEFT, RIGHT, or CENTER.	HTML 3.2
VALIGN="..."	✓ Aligns the text to the TOP, MIDDLE, or BOTTOM.	HTML 3.2
BGCOLOR= "#rrggbb" or *"name"*	Sets background color by rrggbb number or standard color name.	Navigator/ IE
BORDERCOLOR= "#rrggbb" or *"name"*	Specifies border color by rrggbb number or standard color name and must be used with the BORDER attribute.	IE
BORDERCOLOR-DARK="#rrggbb" or *"name"*	Sets independent border color control by rrggbb number or standard color name for one of the two colors used to draw a 3-D border. Must be used with the BORDER attribute.	IE
BORDERCOLOR-LIGHT="#rrggbb" or *"name"*	Sets independent border color control by rrggbb number or standard color name for one of the two colors used to draw a 3-D border. Must be used with the BORDER attribute.	IE
`<TD>...</TD>`	✓ Specifies a standard table data cell.	HTML 3.2
BACKGROUND= "..."	Specifies background image for the table.	IE
ALIGN="..."	✓ Aligns the text to the LEFT, RIGHT, or CENTER.	HTML 3.2
BGCOLOR= "#rrggbb" or *"name"*	Sets background color by rrggbb number or standard color name.	Navigator/ IE
BORDERCOLOR= "#rrggbb" or *"name"*	Specifies border color by rrggbb number or standard color name and must be used with the BORDER attribute.	IE
BORDERCOLOR-DARK="#rrggbb" or *"name"*	Sets independent border color control by rrggbb number or standard color name for one of the two colors used to draw a 3-D border. Must be used with the BORDER attribute.	IE
BORDERCOLOR-LIGHT="#rrggbb" or *"name"*	Sets independent border color control by rrggbb number or standard color name for one of the two colors used to draw a 3-D border. Must be used with the BORDER attribute.	IE
COLSPAN=n	✓ Specifies how many columns of the table this cell should span.	HTML 3.2

(continued)

Table A-7 (continued)

Markup	Description	Reference or Usage
NOWRAP	✓ Indicates that the lines within this cell cannot be broken to fit in the cell.	HTML 3.2
ROWSPAN=n	✓ Specifies how many rows of the table this cell should span.	HTML 3.2
VALIGN=". . ."	✓ Controls vertical alignment within the cell. Values are TOP, MIDDLE, BOTTOM.	HTML 3.2
WIDTH="n"	✓ Describes the cell width in terms of the number of pixels, or the percentage of the table width.	HTML 3.2
HEIGHT="n"	✓ Describes the cell height in terms of the number of pixels.	HTML 3.2
<TH>. . .</TH>	✓ Specifies a table header.	HTML 3.2
BACKGROUND="URL"	Specifies background image for the cell.	IE
ALIGN=". . ."	✓ Aligns the text to the LEFT, RIGHT, or CENTER.	HTML 3.2
BGCOLOR= "#rrggbb" or "name"	Sets background color by rrggbb number or standard color name.	Navigator/ IE
BORDERCOLOR= "#rrggbb" or "name"	Specifies border color by rrggbb number or standard color name and must be used with the BORDER attribute.	IE
BORDERCOLOR- DARK="#rrggbb" or "name"	Sets independent border color control by rrggbb number or standard color name for one of the two colors used to draw a 3-D border. Must be used with the BORDER attribute.	IE
BORDERCOLOR- LIGHT="#rrggbb" or "name"	Sets independent border color control by rrggbb number or standard color name for one of the two colors used to draw a 3-D border. Must be used with the BORDER attribute.	IE
COLSPAN=n	✓ Specifies how many columns of the table this cell should span.	HTML 3.2
NOWRAP	✓ Indicates that the lines within this cell cannot be broken to fit in the cell.	HTML 3.2
ROWSPAN=n	✓ Specifies how many rows of the table this cell should span.	HTML 3.2
VALIGN=". . ."	✓ Controls vertical alignment within the cell. Values are TOP, MIDDLE, BOTTOM.	HTML 3.2

Markup	Description	Reference or Usage
`WIDTH="n"`	✓ Describes the cell width in terms of the number of pixels, or the percentage of the table width.	HTML 3.2
`HEIGHT="n"`	✓ Describes the cell height in terms of the number of pixels.	HTML 3.2
`<THEAD>. . .` `</THEAD>`	Defines table heading row for use in Internet Explorer.	IE
`ALIGN=". . ."`	Aligns the text to the LEFT, RIGHT, or CENTER.	IE
`VALIGN=". . ."`	Controls vertical alignment within the cell. Values are TOP, MIDDLE, BOTTOM.	IE
`<TBODY>. . .` `</TBODY>`	Creates section within table for use in Internet Explorer.	IE
`<TFOOT>. . .` `</TFOOT>`	Defines table footer row for use in Internet Explorer.	IE
`<COLGROUP>. . .` `</COLGROUP>`	Sets properties for columns within Internet Explorer tables.	IE
`HALIGN=". . ."`	Aligns the text to the LEFT, RIGHT, or CENTER.	IE
`VALIGN=". . ."`	Controls vertical alignment within the cell. Values are TOP, MIDDLE, BOTTOM.	IE
`WIDTH="n"`	Indicates width of columns in group for Internet Explorer tables.	IE
`SPAN=n`	Specifies number of contiguous columns in group to which properties should apply.	IE

Table A-8   *Form Markup*

Note: To implement forms, you must be using an HTTP server that supports those options. Check with your server administrator for the complete details.

Markup	Description	Reference or Usage
`<FORM . . .>` `. . . </FORM>`	✓ Encloses the entire form.	HTML 2.0
`ACTION=". . ."`	✓ Identifies what should happen to the data if the form is submitted to a gateway program.	HTML 2.0

(continued)

Table A-8 *(continued)*

Markup	Description	Reference or Usage
`ENCTYPE="..."`	✓ Identifies MIME type of form data.	HTML 2.0
`METHOD="..."`	✓ Identifies methods. Valid options are GET or POST, and one or the other is required.	HTML 2.0
`TARGET="..."`	✓ Specifies the target frame for the forms to appear in if you're using framed pages.	Frames
`onSubmit="..."`	Calls script (JavaScript or VBScript) event if form is submitted.	Script
`<INPUT...>`	✓ Identifies an input field.	HTML 2.0
`onBlur="..."`	Calls script (JavaScript or VBScript) event if reader moves out of field.	Script
`onChange="..."`	Calls script (JavaScript or VBScript) event if user changes field.	Script
`onClick="..."`	Calls script (JavaScript or VBScript) event if user clicks in field.	Script
`onFocus="..."`	Calls script (JavaScript or VBScript) event if user moves into field.	Script
`onSelect="..."`	Calls script (JavaScript or VBScript) event if user selects field.	Script
`ALIGN="..."`	✓ Aligns the text to the TOP, MIDDLE, BOTTOM, LEFT, RIGHT.	HTML 3.2
`CHECKED`	✓ Shows which item is selected by default (checkboxes/radio buttons).	HTML 2.0
`MAXLENGTH=n`	✓ Indicates the maximum number of characters in the field.	HTML 2.0
`NAME="..."`	✓ Indicates the name of the field.	HTML 2.0
`SIZE=n`	✓ Displays a field n characters wide.	HTML 2.0
`SRC="URL"`	Specifies URL address of image to be used if TYPE=IMAGE.	HTML 3.2
`TYPE="..."`	✓ Indicates the type of field. Valid types are TEXT, PASSWORD, CHECKBOX, RADIO, SUBMIT, RESET, IMAGE, HIDDEN, FILE and IMAGE (new in HTML 3.2).	HTML 2.0
`VALUE="..."`	✓ Indicates the value of the input field (the label for Submit and Reset buttons).	HTML 2.0
`TABINDEX=n`	Specifies sequence number for readers who use the Tab key to maneuver around the page.	IE

Markup	Description	Reference or Usage
NOTAB	Removes field from Tab sequence.	IE
TITLE=". . ."	Specifies extra information to appear with field in Internet Explorer.	IE
`<SELECT. . .>` `. . . </SELECT>`	✓ Provides a list of items to select.	HTML 2.0
MULTIPLE	✓ Indicates that multiple selections are allowed.	HTML 2.0
NAME=". . ."	✓ Indicates the name of the field.	HTML 2.0
SIZE=n	✓ Determines the size of the scrollable list by showing n options.	HTML 2.0
`<OPTION. . .>`	✓ Precedes each item in an option list. The closing `</OPTION>` tag is optional.	HTML 2.0
SELECTED	✓ Identifies which option is selected by default.	HTML 2.0
VALUE=". . ."	✓ Indicates value of the field.	HTML 2.0
`<TEXTAREA. . .>` `. . . </TEXTAREA>`	✓ Encloses a multiline text field. The enclosed text is the value appearing in the field.	HTML 2.0
COLS=n	✓ Indicates the number of columns in the field.	HTML 2.0
NAME=". . ."	✓ Indicates the name of the field.	HTML 2.0
ROWS=n	✓ Indicates the number of rows in the field.	HTML 2.0
`<ISINDEX>`	✓ Indicates the presence of a searchable index.	HTML 2.0
PROMPT=". . ."	✓ Specifies a prompt to be used instead of the default Enter Search Keywords.	HTML 2.0

Table A-9   *Frames and Layers*

Markup	Description	Reference or Usage
`<FRAME>`	✓ Establishes a frame.	Frames
ALIGN=". . ."	Specifies LEFT, CENTER, RIGHT, TOP, BOTTOM for frame alignment.	Frames (IE)
BORDER=n	Specifies width of border in pixels.	Frames (Navigator)
FRAMEBORDER=n	Specifies border (1) or no border (0).	Frames (IE)

(continued)

Table A-9 (continued)

Markup	Description	Reference or Usage
MARGINHEIGHT=n	Specifies margin height for frame in pixels.	Frames (IE)
MARGINWIDTH=n	Specifies margin width for frame in pixels.	Frames (IE)
NAME=". . ."	✓ Provides frame name.	Frames
NORESIZE	✓ Prevents reader from resizing frame.	Frames
SCROLLING= ". . ."	✓ Specifies whether the frame can scroll in terms of YES, NO, or AUTO(matic). YES requires scrollbars; NO prohibits them.	Frames
SRC="URL"	✓ Identifies source file that flows into frame.	Frames
<FRAMESET>… </FRAMESET>	✓ Establishes frame layout.	Frames
BORDER=n	Specifies width of border for all contained frames in pixels.	Frames (Navigator)
BORDERCOLOR= #rrggbb or *"name"*	✓ Specifies color for contained frames.	Frames (Navigator)
COLS="n, n"	✓ Specifies column dimensions in pixels, percentage, or in terms of remaining space. COLS="25%, 100, *".	Frames
FRAMEBORDER=n	Specifies border (1) or no border (0).	Frames (IE)
FRAMESPACING=n	✓ Specifies space between frames in pixels.	Frames (IE)
ROWS="n, n"	✓ Specifies row dimensions in pixels, percentage, or in terms of remaining space. ROWS="25%, 100, *".	Frames
<NOFRAMES>. . . </NOFRAMES>	✓ Specifies area of layout document that is visible to frame-incapable browsers.	Frames
<IFRAME>	Identifies floating frame within HTML document.	IE
ALIGN=". . ."	Specifies LEFT, CENTER, RIGHT, TOP, BOTTOM for frame alignment.	IE
FRAMEBORDER=n	Specifies border (1) or no border (0).	IE
HEIGHT=n	Specifies height for frame in pixels.	IE
MARGINHEIGHT=n	Specifies margin height for frame in pixels.	IE

Markup	Description	Reference or Usage
MARGINWIDTH=n	Specifies margin width for frame in pixels.	IE
NAME=". . ."	Provides frame name.	IE
NORESIZE	Prevents frame from being resized.	IE
SCROLLING= ". . ."	Specifies whether the frame can scroll in terms of YES, NO, or AUTO(matic). Yes requires scrollbars; No prohibits them.	IE
SRC="URL"	Identifies source file that flows into frame.	IE
WIDTH=n	Specifies width of frame in pixels.	IE
<LAYER>. . . </LAYER>	Identifies layer within an HTML document.	Navigator
ABOVE=". . ."	Names layer that lies immediately above the current layer.	Navigator
BACKGROUND="URL"	Specifies URL for background image for layer.	Navigator
BELOW=". . ."	Names layer that lies immediately beneath the current layer.	Navigator
BGCOLOR= #rrggbb or "name"	Specifies color for layer in rrggbb number or standard color name.	Navigator
CLIP=x1,y1,x2,y2	Specifies coordinates of a visible (window) rectangle in a layer. Points outside this rectangle in the layer are not visible.	Navigator
LEFT=x	Specifies the location of the frame left border in pixels from the left edge of the window.	Navigator
NAME=". . ."	Provides name for layer so that it can be referenced from other frame.	Navigator
SRC="URL"	Specifies address for text to fill layer.	Navigator
TOP=y	Specifies the location of the frame top in pixels from the top of the window.	Navigator
VISIBILITY= ". . ."	Specifies visibility of layer in terms of SHOW, HIDE, or INHERIT (from containing layer).	Navigator
WIDTH=n	Specifies number of pixels to right border of layer at which point the text wraps.	Navigator
Z-INDEX=z	Specifies integer for stacking order. Higher numbers go on top.	Navigator
<MULTICOL>. . . </MULTICOL>	Identifies area for multiple columns.	Navigator

(continued)

Table A-9 (continued)

Markup	Description	Reference or Usage
COLS=n	Specifies number of columns.	Navigator
GUTTER=n	Specifies width of gutter (space between columns) in pixels.	Navigator
WIDTH="n"	Specifies overall width of column area in percentage or pixels.	Navigator

Table A-10 **Script**

Markup	Description	Reference or Usage
`<SCRIPT>`. . . `</SCRIPT>`	✓ Marks area for script inclusion in HTML document.	Script
LANGUAGE=". . ."	✓ Specifies scripting language, such as JavaScript or VBScript.	Script
SRC="URL"	✓ Specifies filename (URL) containing the script.	Script
TYPE=". . ."	✓ Specifies MIME type for script.	Script

Table A-11 **Style Sheets (CSS1)**

Markup	Description	Reference or Usage
`<SPAN>`...`</SPAN>`	Marks area of document to which a specific style applies.	CSS1
CLASS=". . ."	Identifies the style class (or type) associated with the tag.	CSS1
STYLE=". . ."	Defines the style for all text associated with the tag.	CSS1
`<STYLE>`. . . `</STYLE>`	Indicates area within document for style definitions.	HTML 3.2
TYPE=". . ."	Specifies MIME type of style sheet.	CSS1
TITLE=". . ."	Specifies additional name for the style definition.	CSS1

Note: All tags within the HTML body can accept the following attributes to apply styles.

Markup	Description	Reference or Usage
CLASS="..."	Identifies the style class (or type) associated with the tag.	CSS1
ID="..."	Identifies the style identification value for this particular instance in the document.	CSS1
STYLE="..."	Defines the style for all text associated with the tag.	CSS1

Table A-12   **Internet Explorer Multimedia Extensions**

Markup	Description	Reference or Usage
<BGSOUND>	Indicates background sounds.	IE
SRC="URL"	Indicates background sounds to play after page is opened. Sounds can be WAV, AU, or MID format.	IE
LOOP="..."	Specifies how many times (number or "INFINITE") a sound plays.	IE
<MARQUEE>	Specifies a scrolling text marquee.	IE
ALIGN="..."	Specifies that the text around the marquee should align with the TOP, MIDDLE, or BOTTOM of the marquee.	IE
BEHAVIOR="..."	Specifies how the text should behave as SCROLL, SLIDE, or ALTERNATE.	IE
BGCOLOR= "#rrggbb" or *"name"*	Specifies a background color for the marquee as an rrggbb number or standard color name.	IE
DIRECTION= "..."	Specifies which direction (LEFT or RIGHT) the text should scroll.	IE
HEIGHT="..."	Specifies the height of the marquee, either in pixels or as a percentage of the screen height.	IE
HSPACE=n	Specifies left and right margins for the outside of the marquee, in pixels.	IE
LOOP="..."	Specifies how many times (number or "INFINITE") a marquee will loop.	IE
SCROLLAMOUNT=n	Specifies the number of pixels between each successive progression of the marquee text.	IE
SCROLLDELAY=n	Specifies the number of milliseconds between each successive draw of the marquee text.	IE

(continued)

Table A-12 (continued)

Markup	Description	Reference or Usage
VSPACE=n	Specifies top and bottom margins for the outside of the marquee in pixels.	IE
WIDTH="n"	Sets the width of the marquee, either in pixels or as a percentage of the screen width.	IE

Table A-13	*Applet Tags*	

Markup	Description	Reference or Usage
`<APPLET>`. . . `</APPLET>`	✓ Inserts a Java Applet in the page, subject to the information provided in additional tags between the opening and closing tags.	HTML 3.2
`ALT="`. . .`"`	✓ Specifies alternative text to display if the applet can't run.	HTML 3.2
`ALIGN="`. . .`"`	✓ Places the applet LEFT, CENTER, RIGHT, TOP, MIDDLE, or BOTTOM in the page.	HTML 3.2
`CODE="`. . .`"`	✓ Identifies the Java applet with a standard URL, either relative or absolute.	HTML 3.2
`CODEBASE="`. . .`"`	✓ Specifies the folder in which the applet is located with a URL. Can be omitted to default to folder in which page is located or if CODE= attribute specifies the complete URL.	HTML 3.2
`DOWNLOAD="`. . .`"`	Specifies image download order for Internet Explorer.	IE
`HEIGHT="`. . .`"`	✓ Specifies the height of the applet in pixels.	HTML 3.2
`HSPACE=n`	✓ Specifies left and right gutter for the outside of the applet in pixels.	HTML 3.2
`NAME="`. . .`"`	✓ Gives a name to the applet so that applets on the same page can talk with one another.	HTML 3.2
`PARAM NAME=`	Gives other information to applet. Name varies or is omitted, depending on applet.	IE
`VSPACE=n`	✓ Controls the vertical space (white space) around the applet in pixels.	HTML 3.2

Markup	Description	Reference or Usage
WIDTH="n"	✓ Describes the applet width in terms of the number of pixels or the percentage of the document width.	HTML 3.2
TITLE=". . ."	Specifies extra information to appear with applet in Internet Explorer.	IE
<PARAM . . .>	✓ Gives parameters (other information) to a Java applet. Place between opening and closing <APPLET> tags.	HTML 3.2
NAME=". . ."	✓ Specifies name of parameter. Actual values depend on the applet.	HTML 3.2
VALUE=". . ."	✓ Specifies value of named parameter. Actual values depend on the applet.	HTML 3.2

Table A-14   **EMBED Tags**

Markup	Description	Reference or Usage
<EMBED . . >	✓ Embeds an object (such as a Shockwave animation) in a Web page.	Navigator/IE
HEIGHT=". . ."	✓ Specifies the height of the embedded object in pixels.	Navigator/IE
NAME=". . ."	✓ Gives a name to the embedded object so other objects within the page can communicate with it.	Navigator/IE
Other parameters	✓ Provide other information to object. Should be specified in the documentation of the object. Usually in form of WORD= "value" where WORD and value are both specified in the documentation.	Navigator/IE
PALETTE= #rrggbb|#rrggbb	✓ Specifies foreground and background colors in rrggbb colors.	Navigator/IE
SRC=". . ."	✓ Identifies address of information or code for the embedded object with a standard (absolute or relative) URL.	Navigator/IE
UNITS=". . ."	✓ Specifies units (PIXELS or EN) for the object.	Navigator/IE
WIDTH=n	✓ Specifies WIDTH for object UNITS.	Navigator/IE

Table A-15	*Object Tags*	

Markup	*Description*	*Reference or Usage*
`<OBJECT>. . .` `</OBJECT>`	✓ Inserts an object in the page, subject to the information provided in additional tags between the opening and closing tags.	IE
`ALT=". . ."`	✓ Specifies alternative text to display if the object cannot be run.	IE
`ALIGN=". . ."`	✓ Places the object within the page. `RIGHT`, `MIDDLE`, and `LEFT` float the object as specified and wrap text around it. `CENTER`, `TOP`, and `BOTTOM` align relative to surrounding text.	IE
`BORDER=n`	✓ Controls the thickness of the border around object in pixels.	IE
`CLASSID=". . ."`	✓ Identifies object. Precise syntax depends on object type.	IE
`CODE=". . ."`	✓ Identifies the object with a standard URL, either relative or absolute.	IE
`CODEBASE="URL"`	✓ Specifies the folder in which the object is located with a URL. Precise syntax depends on object type.	IE
`CODETYPE="URL"`	✓ Specifies the type of object code. Precise syntax depends on object type.	IE
`DATA="URL"`	✓ Specifies source for object data. Precise syntax depends on object type.	IE
`DECLARE`	Declares (enables) object but does not instantiate (activate) it.	IE
`HEIGHT=". . ."`	✓ Specifies the height of the object in pixels.	IE
`HSPACE=n`	✓ Specifies left and right gutter for the outside of the object in pixels.	IE
`NAME=". . ."`	✓ Gives a name to the object so objects on the same page can talk with one another.	IE
`NOTAB`	Excludes object from Tab order in page.	IE
`SHAPES=". . ."`	Specifies shaped links in the object.	IE
`STANDBY=". . ."`	Identifies message to be displayed while object loads.	IE
`TABINDEX=n`	Specifies sequence number for readers who use the Tab key to maneuver around the page.	IE
`TITLE=". . ."`	Specifies extra information to appear with object in Internet Explorer.	IE

Markup	Description	Reference or Usage
TYPE=". . ."	Specifies MIME type for data.	IE
USEMAP="mapname"	Identifies the picture as a client-side imagemap and specifies a MAP to use for acting on the user's clicks.	IE
VSPACE=n	Controls the vertical space (white space) around the object in pixels.	IE
WIDTH=n	Describes the object width in terms of the number of pixels or the percentage of the document width.	IE
<PARAM . . .>	Gives parameters (other information) to a applet. Place between opening and closing <OBJECT> tags.	IE
NAME=". . ."	Specifies name of parameter. Actual values depend on the applet.	IE
VALUE=". . ."	Specifies value of named parameter. Actual values depend on the applet.	IE
VALUETYPE= ". . ."	Specifies type of named parameter. Could be DATA, REF, OBJECT.	IE

Special Symbols

This appendix provides you with symbols that you use to include special characters in an HTML document. If you can type a specific character on your keyboard, you probably don't need to use the corresponding special symbol. If you can't type characters such as a letter with an umlaut by using your keyboard, however, you need to use the symbols provided in this list. Tübingen, for example, becomes Tübingen to come out as Tübingen in an HTML document.

According to the HTML 3.2 standards, the mnemonic name (if available) or numeric codes are equally acceptable, so all newer browsers should reproduce all these entities correctly. If you anticipate that your readers are using older browsers, however, and you make extensive use of special symbols, do a little testing first to make sure that their browsers display the symbols correctly.

Note: Positions 1–31 and 127–159 in Table B-1 are not used in HTML 3.2 — we didn't just forget them.

The following table shows the special symbols you can use and the codes used to create them. You can type some characters and symbols in more than one way. To type the symbol Æ, for example, you can type either `&#198;` (from in the Numeric column) or `&AElig;` (from the Mnemonic column).

Table B-1   *Special Symbols*

Appear As	Numeric	Mnemonic	Description
	`&#32;`		Space
!	`&#33;`		Exclamation mark
"	`&#34;`	`&quot;`	Quotation mark
#	`&#35;`		Number sign
$	`&#36;`		Dollar sign
%	`&#37;`		Percent sign
&	`&#38;`	`&amp;`	Ampersand
'	`&#39;`		Apostrophe
(	`&#40;`		Left parenthesis
)	`&#41;`		Right parenthesis
*	`&#42;`		Asterisk
+	`&#43;`		Plus sign
,	`&#44;`		Comma
-	`&#45;`		Hyphen
.	`&#46;`		Period (full stop)
/	`&#47;`		Solidus (slash)
0	`&#48;`		
1	`&#49;`		
2	`&#50;`		
3	`&#51;`		
4	`&#52;`		
5	`&#53;`		
6	`&#54;`		
7	`&#55;`		
8	`&#56;`		
9	`&#57;`		
:	`&#58;`		Colon
;	`&#59;`		Semicolon

Appear As	Numeric	Mnemonic	Description
<	<	<	Less than
=	=		Equal sign
>	>	>	Greater than
?	?		Question mark
@	@		Commercial "at" sign
A	A		
B	B		
C	C		
D	D		
E	E		
F	F		
G	G		
H	H		
I	I		
J	J		
K	K		
L	L		
M	M		
N	N		
O	O		
P	P		
Q	Q		
R	R		
S	S		
T	T		
U	U		
V	V		
W	W		
X	X		
Y	Y		
Z	Z		
[	[		Left square bracket
\	\		Reverse solidus (backslash)

(continued)

Table B-1 (continued)

Appear As	Numeric	Mnemonic	Description
]	&#93;		Right square bracket
^	&#94;		Caret
_	&#95;		Horizontal bar
`	&#96;		Grave accent
a	&#97;		
b	&#98;		
c	&#99;		
d	&#100;		
e	&#101;		
f	&#102;		
g	&#103;		
h	&#104;		
i	&#105;		
j	&#106;		
k	&#107;		
l	&#108;		
m	&#109;		
n	&#110;		
o	&#111;		
p	&#112;		
q	&#113;		
r	&#114;		
s	&#115;		
t	&#116;		
u	&#117;		
v	&#118;		
w	&#119;		
x	&#120;		
y	&#121;		
z	&#122;		
{	&#123;		Left curly brace
|	|		Vertical bar
}	&#125;		Right curly brace

Appear As	Numeric	Mnemonic	Description
~	&#126;		Tilde
	&#127; – 159;		Not used in HTML 3.2
			Nonbreaking space
¡	&#161;	&iexcl;	Inverted exclamation
¢	&#162;	&cent;	Cent sign
£	&#163;	&pound;	Pound sterling
¤	&#164;	&curren;	General currency sign
¥	&#165;	&yen;	Yen sign
¦	&#166;	&brvbar;	Broken vertical bar
§	&#167;	&sect;	Section sign
¨	&#168;	&uml;	Umlaut (diaeresis)
©	&#169;	&copy;	Copyright
ª	&#170;	&ordf;	Feminine ordinal
«	&#171;	&laquo;	Left angle quote, guillemet left
¬	&#172;	&not;	Not sign
-	&#173;	&shy;	Soft hyphen
®	&#174;	&reg;	Registered trademark
¯	&#175;	&macr;	Macron accent
°	&#176;	&deg;	Degree sign
±	&#177;	&plusmn;	Plus or minus sign
²	&#178;	&sup2;	Superscript two
³	&#179;	&sup3;	Superscript three
´	&#180;	&acute;	Acute accent
µ	&#181;	&micro;	Micro sign
¶	&#182;	&para;	Paragraph sign
·	&#183;	&middot;	Center dot
¸	&#184;	&cedil;	Cedilla
¹	&#185;	&sup1;	Superscript one
º	&#186;	&ordm;	Masculine ordinal
»	&#187;	&raquo;	Right angle quote, guillemet right

(continued)

Table B-1 (continued)

Appear As	Numeric	Mnemonic	Description
1/4	&#188;	&frac14;	Fraction one-fourth
1/2	&#189;	&frac12;	Fraction one-half
3/4	&#190;	&frac34;	Fraction three-fourths
¿	&#191;	&iquest;	Inverted question mark
À	&#192;	&Agrave;	Capital A, grave accent
Á	&#193;	&Aacute;	Capital A, acute accent
Â	&#194;	&Acirc;	Capital A, circumflex accent
Ã	&#195;	&Atilde;	Capital A, tilde
Ä	&#196;	&Auml;	Capital A, diaeresis or umlaut mark
Å	&#197;	&Aring;	Capital A, ring
Æ	&#198;	&AElig;	Capital AE diphthong (ligature)
Ç	&#199;	&Ccedil;	Capital C, cedilla
È	&#200;	&Egrave;	Capital E, grave accent
É	&#201;	&Eacute;	Capital E, acute accent
Ê	&#202;	&Ecirc;	Capital E, circumflex accent
Ë	&#203;	&Euml;	Capital E, diaeresis or umlaut mark
Ì	&#204;	&Igrave;	Capital I, grave accent
Í	&#205;	&Iacute;	Capital I, acute accent
Î	&#206;	&Icirc;	Capital I, circumflex accent
Ï	&#207;	&Iuml;	Capital I, diaeresis or umlaut mark
Ð	&#208;	&ETH;	Capital Eth, Icelandic
Ñ	&#209;	&Ntilde;	Capital N, tilde
Ò	&#210;	&Ograve;	Capital O, grave accent

Appear As	*Numeric*	*Mnemonic*	*Description*
Ó	&#211;	&Oacute;	Capital O, acute accent
Ô	&#212;	&Ocirc;	Capital O, circumflex accent
Õ	&#213;	&Otilde;	Capital O, tilde
Ö	&#214;	&Ouml;	Capital O, diaeresis or umlaut mark
x	&#215;		Multiplication sign
Ø	&#216;	&Oslash;	Capital O, slash
Ù	&#217;	&Ugrave;	Capital U, grave accent
Ú	&#218;	&Uacute;	Capital U, acute accent
Û	&#219;	&Ucirc;	Capital U, circumflex accent
Ü	&#220;	&Uuml;	Capital U, diaeresis or umlaut mark
Y	&#221;	&Yacute;	Capital Y, acute accent
þ	&#222;	&THORN;	Capital THORN, Icelandic
ß	&#223;	&szlig;	Small sharp s, German (sz ligature)
à	&#224;	&agrave;	Small a, grave accent
á	&#225;	&aacute;	Small a, acute accent
â	&#226;	&acirc;	Small a, circumflex accent
ã	&#227;	&atilde;	Small a, tilde
ä	&#228;	&auml;	Small a, diaeresis or umlaut mark
å	&#229;	&aring;	Small a, ring
æ	&#230;	&aelig;	Small ae diphthong (ligature)
ç	&#231;	&ccedil;	Small c, cedilla
è	&#232;	&egrave;	Small e, grave accent
é	&#233;	&eacute;	Small e, acute accent

(continued)

Table B-1 (continued)

Appear As	Numeric	Mnemonic	Description
ê	&#234;	&ecirc;	Small e, circumflex accent
ë	&#235;	&euml;	Small e, diaeresis or umlaut mark
ì	&#236;	&igrave;	Small i, grave accent
í	&#237;	&iacute;	Small i, acute accent
î	&#238;	&icirc;	Small i, circumflex accent
ï	&#239;	&iuml;	Small i, diaeresis or umlaut mark
ð	&#240;	&eth;	Small eth, Icelandic
ñ	&#241;	&ntilde;	Small n, tilde
ò	&#242;	&ograve;	Small o, grave accent
ó	&#243;	&oacute;	Small o, acute accent
ô	&#244;	&ocirc;	Small o, circumflex accent
õ	&#245;	&otilde;	Small o, tilde
ö	&#246;	&ouml;	Small o, diaeresis or umlaut mark
÷	&#247;		Division sign
ø	&#248;	&oslash;	Small o, slash
ù	&#249;	&ugrave;	Small u, grave accent
ú	&#250;	&uacute;	Small u, acute accent
û	&#251;	&ucirc;	Small u, circumflex accent
ü	&#252;	&uuml;	Small u, diaeresis or umlaut mark
´y	&#253;	&yacute;	Small y, acute accent
þ	&#254;	&thorn;	Small thorn, Icelandic
ÿ	&#255;	&yuml;	Small y, diaeresis or umlaut mark

The following symbol is nonstandard. Test with your intended audience before using.

Appear As	Numeric	Mnemonic	Description
TM	™	™	Trademark

The following symbols are nonstandard, but may be useful in some cases. At presstime, they worked with Navigator but not with Explorer. As always, test first with your intended audience.

Appear As	Numeric	Mnemonic	Description
—	—	—	Em dash
–	–	–	En dash

Adapted from Character Entities for ISO Latin-1, © International Organization for Standardization, 1986.

Techie Talk

The Glossary contains an alphabetical listing of peculiar terms used throughout this book. At the end of each description is the number of the part in which you find more information about the word described. Typically, that part is not the only place you find the word, but it's the place where the word is discussed or defined in some detail.

absolute URL

The complete URL that gives all the information necessary to find a file or document on the Internet, including protocol type, system name, pathname, and filename. *See also* Uniform Resource Locator. *See* Part III.

alternative text

Text that's visible in place of images, if the browser can't display the images. *See* Part IV.

anchor (hot spot, hyperlink)

Used to indicate the part of a hypertext link that marks the hot spot (the part that users click). Also used to define an anchor by using the NAME= attribute for intradocument links. *See* Part III.

attribute

Part of an HTML tag that specifies additional information. <BODY>, for example, is a tag, and BGCOLOR=whatever is the attribute that goes within the brackets, such as <BODY BGCOLOR=whatever>. *See* Part II.

browser

The software that you use to view HTML documents. A browser translates the tags into a display that's appropriate for your computer system (for example, <B> makes text **bold**). *See* Part I.

case-insensitive

Disregards the difference between uppercase and lowercase text. Case-insensitive software treats "HTML" and "html" as the same item. Case-sensitive software considers them to be two different words. *See* Part II.

CGI-BIN directory

The directory in which server programs are usually stored on a server. Generally, only server administrators have the access needed to place files in this directory, but you should be able to use the files in the directory. *See* Part VI.

checkbox

Used within a form, checkboxes allow readers to select one or more of the available options. *See* Part VI.

chunking

A method of grouping similar information. Also a method of breaking large pieces of information into smaller, manageable pieces. *See* Part VIII.

clickable image

See imagemap. *See* Part IV.

client-side imagemap

An imagemap controlled by the browser software. *See* Part IV.

closing tag

The second half of a paired HTML tag. The closing tag is exactly like the opening tag, except that it doesn't have attributes and it always starts with a slash (/). <HTML> is an opening tag and </HTML> is a closing tag. *See* Part II.

complete URL

See absolute URL. *See* Part III.

converter

A program that changes data from one format to another. In this book, a converter is usually a program that changes documents from a word-processing format (such as WordPerfect) into HTML. These converters are frequently built into or added to existing word-processing programs. *See* Part I.

counter

A server program that tells how many people have accessed a specific HTML document. *See* Part VI.

defining (an imagemap)

Setting the parts of an image that link to other documents. *See* Part IV.

dithering

Displaying an image at a lower-resolution than that at which the image was created. A photograph with millions of colors is dithered to display on a 256-color system. *See* Part IV.

download

To transfer a file from a server to your computer. (To transfer a file from your computer to the server is called *uploading*.) *See* Part IV.

dynamic information

Information or data on a Web page that changes (or should change) frequently, such as news or weather forecasts. *See* Part VIII.

electronic document

A document that can be read or displayed on a computer — as opposed to a book, which is a paper document. *See* Part I.

external link

Links away from the current HTML document to another document, possibly even elsewhere on the Internet. *See* Part III.

filename

The name for a document on a computer. Most HTML documents have a filename plus an extension of .htm or .html. *See* Part III.

File Transfer Protocol (FTP)

An Internet file transfer program, based on TCP/IP (Transmission Control Protocol/Internet Protocol), that's used to upload or download files. *See* Part I.

folder (also called a directory)

An on-screen container (file folder) that holds files. *See* Part III.

form

The parts of an HTML document that allow readers to respond to questions or provide information. *See* Part VI.

frame

A subdivision of the browser window that contains an HTML document. Frames let you put multiple documents in their own parts of the browser window. *See* Part VII.

frameset document

The specialized HTML document that establishes the structure for frames in a Web site. *See* Part VII.

FTP

See File Transfer Protocol. *See* Part I.

FTP site

A source for data on the Internet. *See* Part III.

GIF

An image file type that's particularly suitable for drawings. GIF images work with almost all Web browsers. GIF images are compressed to make them smaller without losing any information. *See* Part IV.

hierarchical organization

A type of organization used if you have more than one major topic. *See* Part VIII.

home page

A common term for the starting point of an HTML document on the Internet. Many people make a personal home page as their first experiment with HTML. *See* Part VIII.

horizontal rule

A line across HTML documents, created by `<HR>`, that's used to separate different parts of text. *See* Part V.

hostname

The name of a computer on the Internet (generally something like `www.company.com`) that you may be able to access and use. *See* Part III.

hot spot (hyperlink)

A place on a Web page that users can click to connect to other topics, documents, or Web sites. *See* Part III.

HTML (HyperText Markup Language)

Technically, HTML is a variant of SGML (Standard Generalized Markup Language), but for the purposes of this book, it's just the tags that make your Web pages work. *See* Part I.

HTML editor

A specialized program that's used for adding HTML markup tags to a document. You can use BBEdit with HTML Extensions on Macintosh's HotDog or HTMLpad on Windows; and HoTMetaL on Windows, Macintosh, or UNIX, among many programs. *See* Part I.

HTML tags

Bits of text, enclosed within < >, that define different parts of a document. Required by HTML specifications. *See* Part II.

Hyperlink

See *anchor*. *See* Part III.

hyperspace

A mythical area in which linking from page to page takes place. *See* Part VIII.

HyperText

A term for documents that you can read in a nonlinear way. If this Glossary were a HyperText document, you could click a word and zip right to the definition or other definitions that include the word. *See* Part I.

HyperText Markup Language

See *HTML*. *See* Part I.

image

A drawing, picture, or photograph in electronic form. *See* Part IV.

imagemap

Images or parts of images that you click to link to other information. Also called a *clickable image*. *See* Part IV.

internal link

A link that points to another place within the same document. *See also* Uniform Resource Locator. *See* Part III.

Internet

The remarkably overhyped worldwide collection of computer networks that all speak the same language. The World Wide Web is a significant part of the Internet. *See* Part I.

intranet

Similar to the Internet, except that it is corporation-wide rather than worldwide. *See* Part VI.

JPG (or JPEG)

An image file type developed by the Joint Photographic Experts Group that's particularly suitable for photographs. JPG images work with most Web browsers. JPG images are compressed to make them much smaller, but they lose some detail as they're compressed. *See* Part IV.

LAN (local area network)

Provides an avenue for distributing HTML documents within an organization. A LAN can also include a Web server, thus taking a step toward being an intranet. *See* Part I.

linear organization

A type of organization you can use when providing instructions or procedures online. *See* Part VIII.

link

The connection between an anchor and the document or file to which you're linking. *See* Part III.

local area network

See LAN. See Part I.

location line

Enables you to type the specific address to view in the browser. Located toward the top of your browser window. *See* Part III.

lossy

Compression that discards some of the original data contained in the file. It's like packing a suitcase and throwing away anything that doesn't fit instead of just sitting on the suitcase and forcing everything in (as in lossless compression). *See* Part IV.

mapping (an imagemap)

See Defining (an imagemap). See Part IV.

markup language

A collection of tags or codes that tells computers what to do with the text within the tags. These markup languages used to be popular but were supplanted by WYSIWYG (what-you-see-is-what-you-get) editors. Markup languages are now regaining popularity because of their famous sibling, the HyperText Markup Language. *See* Part I.

navigating

The process of moving between or among pages and documents, particularly on the World Wide Web. *See* Part III.

navigation tools

Buttons, links, imagemaps, or anything else that allows readers to go from page to page within your Web site more easily. *See* Part VIII.

nesting

Putting sets of tags within other sets of tags. *See* Part II.

news server

Provides access to Usenet News, a collection of discussion groups on the Internet. You can link HTML documents to these groups. *See* Part III.

online

Refers to being on a computer or on a network, as opposed to being offline (using paper). *See* Part I.

opening tag

The first of a pair of HTML tags. This is the tag that includes all of the attributes. *See also* *paired tag*. *See* Part II.

paired tag

Tags that always come in twos. They have an opening tag, sometimes text in the middle, and a closing tag. *See* Part II.

pixels

The little individual dots that make up images. *See* Part IV.

platform

Indicates the computer and operating system (for example, Windows 95, Macintosh, or OS/2). *See* Part I.

PNG

Portable Network Graphic. A new graphic standard that's, as yet, not widely implemented. *See* Part IV.

Portable Network Graphic

See PNG. See Part IV.

protocol

The standardized language that computers use to transfer information. *See* Part III.

protocol indicator

The first part of a URL. It indicates what kind of computer language the file is written in. The standard protocol indicator on the Web is generally `http://` and points to HTML documents. *See* Part III.

publishing

In this context, putting HTML documents on a server for other people to see and read. *See* Part I.

radio button

A button within a form that enables you to make only one selection — similar to buttons on your car radio. *See* Part VI.

reader profile

Describes your typical readers, including what information they already have, what they need, and what they don't care about. *See* Part VIII.

relative URL

A URL that points to another file in relation to the location of the current one. Compare 2345 N. Gray St. (absolute) with "down the street and to the left" (relative). *See also Uniform Resource Locator. See* Part III.

RGB number

The number, often hexadecimal, that indicates the relative amounts of red, blue, and green that are used to make a specific color. *See* Part IV.

scanning

Occurs if the reader's purpose is to see what information is available in a document. *See* Part VIII.

select list

A list on a form from which you can select one or more items by clicking the items. The font selection list in your word processing program is a good example of this type of list. *See* Part VI.

server

A computer that provides files or documents on request to other computers. Also known as HTML Server, HTTP Server, or Web Server. *See* Part I and Part VI.

server program

A small program that provides information to the server or that does something on command from a browser, such as take the output from a form. *See* Part VI.

server-side imagemap

An imagemap controlled by the server software. *See* Part IV.

server-side include

A command that tells the server to include other information with a document being served. Think of it as the waiter grabbing the ketchup on the way to your table. *See* Part VI.

skimming

Occurs if the reader's purpose is to look for specific information within a document. *See* Part VIII.

static information

Information on a Web page that doesn't often change, such as an address. *See* Part VIII.

structure tag

An HTML tag that doesn't show (visibly) in a document but tells browsers about the document. *See* Part II.

surfing the net

Perusing the interesting or inane information that is available on the World Wide Web. *See* Part I.

tag

A command that's used in a markup language. In HTML, tags are enclosed in brackets (< >). *See* Part II.

testing

Trying out your HTML document to make sure that it works as it should. *See* Part VIII.

text

In the sense of HyperText, includes text, graphics, and anything else you choose to cram into your HTML documents. *See* Part I.

text area

A part of an HTML form that gives users a place to type longer chunks (several columns by several rows) of information. *See* Part VI.

text editor

Any computer program that can save plain-text documents. Examples include SimpleText for Macintosh, Notepad for Windows, and pico for UNIX. *See* Part I.

thumbnail

Small image used to represent a large image, particularly if the smaller image links to the larger image. *See* Part VI.

transparent background

An image that doesn't have a background color that shows up in the browser. *See* Part IV.

Uniform Resource Locator (URL)

The address of a document on the Internet that's generally used for specifying addresses for HTML documents. *See* Part III.

URL

See Uniform Resource Locator. See Part III.

Usenet News

See news server. *See* Part III.

validation service

A service on the Internet to check your HTML documents for compliance with the HTML specifications. *See* Part VIII.

virtual domain

A domain name (such as www.raycomm.com) that actually resides on a different computer (as ours resides on www.xmission.com). *See* Part VI.

Web

The interlocking maze of HTML documents, all related resources and media, and the links among them on the Internet. *See* Part I.

Web server

See server. *See* Part I and Part VI.

Web server administrator

See Webmaster. *See* Part VI.

Web site

A page or set of pages at a particular organization. Also used to refer to a set of HTML documents. *See* Part VIII.

webbed organization

A type of organization used to let readers cross-reference other topics easily. *See* Part VIII.

Webmaster

The person or people who maintain a Web site. *See* Part VI.

World Wide Web (WWW)

See Web. *See* Part I.

x,y coordinates

Specifies the number of pixels down and to the right from the top left corner of an image. *See* Part IV.

Index

B

<B> (boldface) tag, 26, 33, 180
BACKGROUND attribute,
    94–95, 176, 183, 185,
    186, 191
background color
    adding, 24, 92
    in transparent images, 63–64
    for Web pages, 92–94, 97
    Web site theme consider-
        ations, 162
backslash (\), 201
banner document, 143
Bare Bones Software, 15
<BASE> (base) tag, 175
<BASEFONT> (standard font)
    tag, 180
BBEdit HTML editor, 15
BEHAVIOR attribute, 193
BELOW attribute, 191
BGCOLOR attribute
    for color background, 92
    example, 24
    frames and layers
        markup, 191
    with <MARQUEE> (marquee)
        tag, 193
    structural markup, 176
    table markup, 183, 185, 186
BGPROPERTIES attribute, 176
<BGSOUND> (background
    sounds) tag, 193
<BIG> (big text) tag, 180
black background, for Web
    pages, 93
blank lines
    in tables, 112
    in text, 25
<BLINK> (blinking text)
    tag, 180
<BLOCKQUOTE> (block
    quote) attribute, 38–40,
    177
<BODY> (body) tag
    with background color
        attribute, 94
    described, 27, 29, 177–178
boldface tag, 26, 33, 180
BORDER attribute
    with <FRAME> tag, 149, 189
    with <FRAMESET> tag, 146,
        148, 190
    with <IMG> tag, 56, 70, 182
    with <OBJECT> (insert
        object) tag, 195

    with <TABLE> (table) tag,
        110, 111, 183
BORDERCOLOR attribute, 146,
    183, 185, 186, 190
BORDERCOLORDARK
    attribute, 184, 185, 186
BORDERCOLORLIGHT
    attribute, 184, 185, 186
borders
    appearance, 70
    creating, 56
    removing, 71
    for tables, 110, 111
borrowing images, 62
bottom alignment, images,
    73, 76
bottom-navigation tool, 168

 (break line) tag,
    106–107, 131, 133, 139
brackets [, 202
breaking
    lines of text, 106–107,
        131, 133
    Web pages with horizontal
        rules, 107–109
browsers
    clickable images and, 79–80
    copying Web page
        backgrounds, 94
    described, 15–17, 210
    disregarding formatting, 25,
        26, 28, 35
    finding closing tags, 24
    formatting commands
        and, 102
    frames and, 143, 145,
        147–148, 152–153
    identifying document
        characteristics, 26
    images and, 56, 58, 60, 62
    location line, 51
    referencing documents, 28
    relative URLs and, 45
    tables and, 109
    text alignment and, 100–102
    viewing HTML documents,
        2, 3, 15–17, 27
bulleted lists. *See also* <UL>
        (unordered list) tag
    for "at-a-glance" infor-
        mation, 165
    attributes for, 38, 174, 179
buttons
    on forms, 125–126
    as navigation tool for Web
        sites, 167

C

capitalization
    in directory names, 44
    for HTML tags, 25
CAPTION attribute, 184
caret (^), 202
case insensitivity, 25, 210
CELLPADDING attribute, 184
cells, in tables, 110, 111
CELLSPACING attribute, 184
Center for High Energy
    Physics, 11
centering
    horizontal rules, 107–109
    text, 100–102
cgi-bin directory, 118, 121,
    210. *See also* Web
    servers
CHARSET attribute, 176
checkboxes, on forms,
    126–129, 210
CHECKED attribute, 125,
    129, 188
chunking information, with
    lists, 166, 211
circles, in imagemaps, 82,
    83–84
<CITE> (citation) tag, 180
CLASS attribute, 192
CLASSID attribute, 195
CLEAR attribute, 106–107,
    177, 184
"Click here," avoiding, 49
clickable images, 79–89,
    164, 210
client-side imagemap, 79,
    80, 211
CLIP attribute, 191
clip-art libraries, 19, 62
closing HTML tag, 24, 211
<CODE> (mark computer
    source code), 180
CODE attribute, 194, 196
CODEBASE attribute, 194, 196
code-based HTML editors, 14,
    15. *See also* HTML
    editors
CODETYPE attribute, 196
<COL> (column) tag, 187
<COLGROUP> (properties for
    columns) tag, 187
colon (:), 200
COLOR attribute, 102, 105,
    178, 180
color palettes, 60